Gertrude E. Carpenter
417 Second Ave.
Dixon, Illinois 61021

Evelyn Ruth Chase

Marc Carpenter —
With Appreciation —
Sincerely
[signature]
11/187

On behalf of the Board of Directors, officers and
employees of Dixon National Bank, we are pleased to present
to our customers and friends this limited edition copy of
DIXON: A PICTORIAL HISTORY

We hope this beautifully illustrated and well-documented
volume will prove to be a cherished addition to your family
library as well as a rare collector's item in years to come.

Dixon National Bank is proud to have played a vital,
long-standing role in our community's heritage and growth.

We dedicate this book to the people of Dixon
- past and present - whose faith, determination and courage
helped to build a strong foundation for our city's progress
and growth - and in so doing made it a find place to live,
work and play.

Donald R. Lovett

Donald R. Lovett
*President and
Chairman of the Board*
DIXON NATIONAL BANK

PRESENTED BY DIXON NATIONAL BANK

DIXON
A Pictorial History

By

GEORGE LAMB

G. Bradley Publishing, Inc.
St. Louis, Missouri

DIXON

A PICTORIAL HISTORY

by George Lamb

A Limited Edition
of 2000
of which this is

NUMBER __383__

PUBLICATION STAFF:
   AUTHOR: George Lamb
   ADVISORS: Stella Grobe
             Mary Ellen Wilson
             Bud Wilson
             Jeff Lovett
             John Kuster
   COVER ARTIST: Judy Dixon
   BOOK DESIGN: IPC Graphics
   COPY EDITOR: Gloria Baraks
   PUBLISHER: G. Bradley Publishing, Inc.
   SPONSOR: Dixon National Bank

All photographs, unless otherwise noted, are from the collections of the *Dixon Telegraph*, the Dixon Public Library, the Loveland Community House Museum and Jeffrey A. Lovett.

First Edition 1987

Copyright © 1987 by G. Bradley Publishing, Inc. All Rights Reserved. Printed in the United States of America. No part of this publication my be reproduced, stored in a retrieval system, or transmitted, in any form or by any means, electronic, mechanical, photocopying, recording, or otherwise, without the prior written permission of the publisher.

ISBN 0-943963-00-1
Printed in the United States of America

TABLE OF CONTENTS

Foreword 7

Chapter I: Early Years 1830 - 1859 9

Chapter II: Expansion Years 1860 - 1889 27

Chapter III: Growth Years 1890 - 1929 67

Chapter IV: Changing Years 1930 - 1959 133

Chapter V: Modern Years 1960 - Present 171

Acknowledgements 196

Bibliography 197

Index 198

DIXON NATIONAL BANK

BOARD OF DIRECTORS

Ray H. Neisewander, Jr.

Thomas D. Shaw   Gary R. Gehlbach   Warren E. Walder   Walter C. Knack, Jr.
James P. Green   Donald R. Lovett, Chairman   Richard E. Lovett

FOREWORD

Nothing but a small log cabin and a crude log raft greeted John Dixon, his wife Rebecca and their family that long ago spring day in 1830. The rushing river, tall timber and dense undergrowth that stretched back to the open lush prairie lands beyond were beautiful to the eye. This was the place John Dixon had chosen as his home, the place he would spend the next 46 years of his life. The rich land, abundant natural resources and constant flow of water providing unlimited power were the foundation of a dynamic community. Dixon and other farsighted entrepreneurs developed the city's future and brought prominence to the central city in Northern Illinois.

Over the years, the diversity and character of its people would provide a solid foundation for the city of Dixon. From workers to executives, from mothers and housewives to merchants, professionals and educators, Dixon residents have served, taught and led their community to the forefront of accomplishment.

In the pages of *Dixon: A Pictorial History,* Dixon comes alive through photographs which serve as windows to the past. These many pictures and the text surrounding them enable readers to share in the excitement and vitality of the city's development. Well-documented by local history buff, George Lamb, *Dixon: A Pictorial History* is a book full of history, legend and lore to be cherished forever.

JOHN DIXON

The son of a British soldier who had remained in America after the Revolutionary War, John Dixon was born in the village of Rye, Westchester County, New York, October 9, 1784. When 21 years old, he moved to New York City where he became the proprietor of a clothing store and merchant tailoring establishment. Untiring in efforts for the promotion of temperance and religious interests, Dixon was one of the active members and directors of the "Young Men's Bible Society of the City of New York."

After 15 years of residence in New York City, Dixon's doctor found symptons of pulmonary disease in his patient and advised a change in climate. Dixon immediately sold his business and home and started his westward trek.

The Dixon family left New York in a covered wagon drawn by a single horse and traveled west to Pittsburgh. There they engaged a flatboat and floated down the Ohio River to Shawneetown, Illinois, where they disembarked. A cross country trip north brought them to Fancy Creek near Springfield, Illinois. After a few years, John Dixon and his family moved further north and settled in Fort Clark (Peoria).

Later, Dixon moved further north to Bureau County and in 1830, made one more journey to settle along the banks of the Rock River for the rest of his life. John Dixon, his wife, Rebecca, and their five children arrived at Ogee's Ferry in April, 1830.

In the years following, "Father" Dixon (a title bestowed in deference to both his age and the fact that he founded the city that to this day carries his name) served as interpreter and trader with the local Indians, council to U.S. Army officers during the Black Hawk War of 1832, Postmaster, first village president and a host of other duties both occupational and honorary.

"Father" Dixon, in 1838, offered a square block of "high and clear" ground within the limits of Dixon's Ferry for the construction of a court house. He also donated 80 acres of farmland to the newly formed Lee County in 1839 so that funds could be realized for the construction of the governmental facility.

Named *Nada-chu-ra-sak* by the Winnebago Indians due to his "long white hair," Dixon platted an 80-acre site on the north side of the Rock River in 1840 and later, gave a block square piece of land to local citizens living on the north side as a public park.

After 1836, "Father" Dixon lived on a farm south and west of Dixon and, 17 years later, with a daughter-in-law in a northside home near the Rock River. For many years, Indians traveling through the area would stop to visit Dixon and reminisce about a time rapidly passing them all by.

In 1901, a writer who had known "Father" Dixon personally looked back on his life and commented:

"Father Dixon was a man of refined instincts and cultured mind. Of most kindly nature, the very soul of honor and with a broadly sympathetic heart, he was recognized as a true friend by the well disposed, alike among the white settlers and the redskins who venerated him as a great chief. But while his mild blue eyes beamed with kindness, the firm set of his lips indicated that there was in his moral make-up no compromise with principle."

At the time of his death on July 6, 1876, Dixon could look back over a life of accomplishment and realize the tiny roughhewn little hamlet along the banks of the Rock River had grown into a thriving, bustling midwestern community.

Organized on January 29, 1853, the First Presbyterian Church in Dixon, meeting in rented quarters, selected as its initial pastor, Reverend W.W. Harsha. Reverend Harsha and his family, pictured here, resided in Dixon until 1862.

CHAPTER I

EARLY

YEARS

1830 - 1859

When the last of the great glaciers melted, the Rock River cut its present valley southwestward to the Mississippi River leaving in its wake not only the great bend at Grand Detour, but some of the most beautiful river valley land and scenery in Illinois.

The early Indian tribes inhabiting the Rock River area thrived on its rich soil, vast forests, luxurious vegetation, abundant wild game and peaceful serenity. Natives of the Sac, Fox, Winnebago, Pottawatomie, Illinois and other tribes traveled through the valley area settling for a period of time before moving on again.

The first white men to traverse the area were the very early explorers who paved the way for others to follow. The 1673 journey of Marquette and Jolliet through the Illinois country gave the French a claim to the area. In 1749, when the Ohio Company was chartered by King George II of England, the British took title to all the land in the rich river valleys.

The first white man of record in the Dixon area was a Frenchman, Pierre LaPorte. His stay was long, from 1780 to 1810, and his dealing with the local Indians amicable and always honorable.

Another Frenchman, La Sallier, came to the region in 1793 and later married a girl from either the Pottawatomie or Winnebago Indian tribe. Some historians claim Joseph Ogee, the man who sold his river crossing business to John Dixon in 1830, married a daughter of this union, his wife, Madeline.

Throughout the early 1800's, large numbers of settlers from the east began to move into southern Illinois. Travel along the Ohio River westward and northward along the Mississippi, Wabash and Illinois Rivers made it comparatively easy to reach the new territory.

Prior to 1818, Illinois had experienced Spanish feudalism, French imperialism and English colonialism; none of which either had the time nor secured the interests of the people for a system of government to settle its roots.

It's development, rather, waited for the coming of a democratic people seeking a new way of life and leadership unencumbered by political philosophies and systems originating in the Middle Ages.

The French (who didn't recognize the British claim) and the British (who had laid a rather late claim to the area after years of concentrating their efforts on the Atlantic seaboard colonies) soon went to war over the western part of the rapidly emerging new country.

When the British finally defeated the French and established the Northwest Territory of which Illinois was a large part, a growing tide of emigrants came to Illinois who not only wanted new lands but a new way of government under which to live.

In the next 40 years (1778 - 1818) the population of Illinois had grown to over 40,000 people; mostly Southerners of Scotch, Irish and English descent from Kentucky, Tennessee, the Carolinas and Virginia. Illinois was granted statehood status on December 3, 1818, and admitted to the Federal Union of States by proclamation of President James Madison.

As more and more emigrants traveled north in Illinois to settle on its vast rich prairie lands, river crossings became of increasing importance to the future growth of the state. The natural obstacle a river presented had to be overcome; an important factor in the establishment of Dixon in the heart of northern Illinois.

The early life of the French-Canadian trader, trapper and interpreter, Joseph Ogee, is clouded in the mists of history. First records of Fort Clark (Peoria) place him in that vicinity in the 1820's when he was employed by the American Fur Company as their agent at a yearly salary of $3,000.

Joseph and Madeline Ogee met John Dixon when both were active in the life of Fort Clark. In 1827, a mutual friend, John L. Bogardus, attempted to establish a ferry crossing over the Rock River. His efforts met with failure.

In the spring of the next year, 1828, Joseph Ogee moved north from Fort Clark to take over the river crossing calling his business enterprise Ogee's Ferry. At the same time, John Dixon and his family traveled northward to settle at Boyd's Grove in Bureau County. Dixon's move was central to a mail carrying contract he had recently received allowing him to deliver government mail between Galena and Fort Clark.

Two years later, on April 11, 1830, the John Dixon family arrived at Ogee's Ferry to move into the established cabin and take over the Rock River ferry crossing. Ogee's operation of the riverside business had been an increasing failure with the result that Dixon purchased his entire business operation. Dixon soon enlarged the log cabin with a two-story addition and began a successful trading business with neighboring Indians and traveling hunters, trappers and military men.

The period of the Black Hawk War of 1832 passed with the Dixon cabin being the only dwelling located at Dixon's Ferry. But, following that senseless struggle between Black Hawk and his Indian followers and the Army of volunteer militiamen and regular Army soldiers, overland travel once again began.

In 1835, John Dixon recorded his 40-acre plat of the Town of Dixon covering the south side of the Rock River. The next year the "Town of Oporto" was begun. This was a land speculation on the north side of the Rock River that was doomed to failure. In 1842, eighty acres east of the Oporto territory was platted by Dixon to be called North Dixon.

The fall of 1836 saw the tiny village of Dixon consisting of four log cabins, a frame house, a blacksmith shop and two or three houses in the process of construction.

Log houses were those of "Father" John Dixon, Colonel Samuel L. Johnson's that also served as a boardinghouse and one built by Dr. Forrest at the corner of Water (River) Street and Ottawa Avenue. In a room about ten-feet square, built as a lean-to, was the village post office headquarters of "Father" Dixon.

The frame house, occupied by Jude W. Hamilton, was opposite James Dixon's cabin that stood until 1876. The blacksmith shop was in a log structure just a few yards east of the lean-to post office. In it a bachelor, John Wilson, worked and lived.

At this time, "Father" Dixon lived on his farm in what is now the Dementtown area of the city. Six families resided in Dixon headed by James P. Dixon, Peter McKenney, Samuel L. Johnson, Jude W. Hamilton, James B. Barr and E.W. Hine. The single men were Dr. Oliver Everett (who was to doctor the ills and injuries of the city's citizens for over 50 years), Smith Gilbraith, Daniel B. McKenney and John Wilson.

In 1837, the first dry goods store in Dixon opened. Operated as S.M. Bowman Company, the building the business occupied was located at the corner of River and Galena. The building later housed the Pheonix Hotel and a store owned by Stiles and Eddy. It burned in a raging fire in the winter of 1846.

The year 1837 also saw the beginning of the long history of the Nachusa House as it is known today. The Dixon Hotel Company was organized in that year and in 1840, the Dixon Hotel or Dixon House was built on First Street. In 1852, the structure was moved to Galena Avenue. In March, 1853, after years of waiting, the Nachusa House was finally finished and formally opened to the public on December 10th with Jerome Porter as its first landlord.

The establishment of Lee County, with Dixon as its county seat and location of its courthouse, on February 27, 1839 gave the Rock River city yet another avenue to future growth.

"Father" Dixon continued his ferry boat river crossing (charging the princely sum of "25¢ per man and horse") until 1846 when the first bridge across the Rock River was constructed.

The 1840's and 1850's brought a steady growth to Dixon with commerical and industrial expansion continuing to grow on a healthy economic base. Settlers arrived daily from the south and east; some staying only long enough to rest on their way west and north, others settling down to become permanent Dixon citizens.

By 1850, Dixon had grown to 1,073 people, a figure that doubled in the next decade and grew further to almost 8,000 in 1900. Sixty years later a population of 10,565 was realized.

The beginning of the *Dixon Telegraph* and *Lee County Herald* marked the start of a 136-year publishing affiliation with the community. Charles R. Fisk, editor and owner, employed the services of B.F. Shaw to publish the first newspaper on May 1, 1851.

Commerical development continued through the next two decades as taverns, stores, mills, and hotels were constructed in the riverside city. The first regular tavern was built by Peter McKenney and H. Thompson on Hennepin Avenue. Later known as the Mansion House, the Huntley House and finally, the Western Hotel, the facility remained a part of Dixon until the early 1900's.

Further development of Dixon proceeded and on May 1, 1853, West Dixon was platted followed by Stedman's Addition in 1854. John Dement's large tracts of land in the western section of Dixon, later to be known as Dementtown, were platted in the same year. Both the Shabbona House (1856) and the Dement House (1857) served the railroad business of Dixon for many years in the Dementtown vicinity.

Industry was as important a segment of Dixon life as any other facet. When the Illinois Central Railroad finally arrived in 1855, the various factories in the growing community expanded to meet the needs of more and more people. The ICRR was a result of the Illinois Land Grant Act of 1850 that saw a 705½ mile railroad system from Cairo to East Dubuque with an additional line to Chicago become a reality within five years.

Lumber and flour mills, a cooperage firm and the Dixon Plow Works of 1854 all led to a strong industrial picture for Dixon. The large five-story flour mill operated by Brooks, Dement and Daley began grinding corn in December, 1853. The mill, built at a cost of $15,000, was sold six years later to C. Godfrey and Sons and became known as the Farmer's Mills.

Local industry depended primarily on river and cross-country traffic in the early years and later, on the railroads that passed through the country. The railroad's arrival in Dixon allowed local products to be distributed across the nation.

Churches and schools were of prime importance to early Dixon settlers in the era prior to the Civil War. The earliest local church was the Methodist Church that first held meetings in 1837 on the second floor of Bowman and Boardman's Store.

Early 1838 saw the First Baptist Church begin followed later in the same year by the Episcopal Church. Another protestant church organized early in the city's history was the Lutheran Church begun in 1848 serving a total of 16 persons in its congregation. The 25 Catholic families who had been added to Dixon's population by 1854 were the original members of the church when St. Patrick's parish was initiated in the community.

Schools offered a civilizing influence on early-day communities like Dixon. Not only important to the educational betterment of the city, initial schools contributed a dual function as public meeting places.

John K. Robinson, who had first visited Dixon's Ferry during the Black Hawk War of 1832, stayed in the area after the Indian war had ceased. Robinson was a brother-in-law of "Father" Dixon and a man with an above-average education for that time. He taught the Dixon children in the family log cabin and became, therefore, the village's first schoolteacher.

Early efforts at education led to classes being conducted in the Dixon cabin by John K. Robinson and later, in the Methodist Church building. In 1838, with the construction of a new First Baptist Church, grade school classes were conducted in both buildings.

Dixon's first public place of learning was built during the summer of 1837, about a block from the present site of Oakwood Cemetery. A total of $515 was raised locally to construct a building that was "perfectly plain, without a cornice and enclosed with undressed oak siding and a hardwood roof." A two-room affair heated by a large box stove, it was moved several blocks east along Ottawa Avenue in 1839.

The Dixon Collegiate Institute, founded in 1855 by the Rock River Presbytery, at first used rented space for classes. The institute's building, when constructed, overlooked the Rock River at Bluff Park and was one of the most prominent features of Dixon's early skyline.

A public high school was established in Dixon in 1858 in the basement of the Methodist Church and by 1859, this school had five departments and about 400 students.

Dixon commercial, industrial, educational and religious endeavors continued to expand and become strong. The population flourished as the name of the community was changed from Dixon's Ferry to the Village of Dixon to the Town of Dixon by 1843. On March 1, 1853, an election was held whereby elected trustees were chosen to run the governmental affairs of the city. These trustees elected "Father" John Dixon as their first President.

In the thirty years since "Father" John Dixon and his family arrived at the ferry boat crossing over the Rock River, the city that bore his name had grown with a constant pattern of expansion to the point where its roots were firmly entrenched in the rich soil boarding the passing river. The tiny hamlet that had once been only a single log cabin entity in 1830 was yet to see its full destiny revealed as the major community in the heart of the Rock River Valley.

DIXON PURCHASED

In April, 1830, the French-Canadian ferry boat operator, Joseph Ogee, owned the land, tavern, trading post and river-crossing ferry operation that formed the nucleus of what is now the city of Dixon. In that month John Dixon purchased all of Ogee's property and assets for a total of $550.

Ogee had moved into the Rock River valley area in 1827 having lived before that date in the Fort Clark (Peoria) area. His trading post and river-crossing business grew to the point that by 1829, he decided to take in a partner. This was done with a man named George Skellenger of Galena for a price of $700.

The initial record of Ogee's sale of his property to John Dixon is recorded in a deed filed in the spring of 1832 in Galena, the county seat of Jo Daviess County. This deed notes that Ogee sold "all my rightful title, interest and claim of, in and to the improvements, ferry and appurtenances at or near the place usually known as Ogee's Ferry on Rock River to John Dixon."

Mention in this deed between Dixon and Ogee is made of a March, 1830 mortgage given to G. Skellenger. In speaking of the mortgage, Ogee notes "which I do not bind myself to prevent the operation of and to release to Dixon all rents and undertakings."

For all practical purposes, this removed Skellenger from the picture.

John Dixon took over Ogee's property on April 11, 1830, and immediately began to make improvements upon it. However, it wasn't until about two years later that Ogee's deed to Dixon was filed.

The deed, filed in Book A, Page 163 and 164, March 1, 1832, by J.E. Stevenson, recorder, for "a fee for recording, 95 cents" notes:

> "In consideration of the foregoing the said Dixon has given me his two several notes for the sum of $400, payable in four months after this date."

This deed, then, officially changed the ownership of Lots 5 and 6, Block 7, in the original town of Dixon from the hands of the early settler, Joseph Ogee, to the management of John Dixon. And all for only $550.

JOHN DIXON'S LOG HOME

When John Dixon and his family arrived at Ogee's Ferry on April 11, 1830, they took over the log structure formerly occupied by the French-Canadian, Joseph Ogee. This log cabin was too small for the seven Dixons, so the immediate addition of a double cabin was begun.

The log cabin structure faced south at a slight angle to the Rock River and was directly in front of the road leading south to Fort Clark (Peoria) and north to Galena.

The rough log addition was quickly completed as was a "block house" section of the original cabin making half of it two stories high with a pitched roof. Later additions to the log cabin structure made it over ninety-feet in length. The blockhouse section and cabin section were connected together and covered with split shakes giving it a more lasting look.

During the Black Hawk War of 1832, a Mr. Tilson used part of the cabin as the Army's suttler and trader. In the winter of 1833-34, the room was devoted to a schoolhouse where John K. Robinson taught the first school lessons to the Dixon children.

"Father" John Dixon's cabin was destroyed in 1845 according to local history reports. The site of the community's first dwelling is today commemorated by a marker placed by the Dixon Chapter of the Daughters of the American Revolution in 1901. It is located at the corner of West First Street and Peoria Avenue.

BLACK HAWK

An Indian war-leader, born at Saukenauk in 1767, was later to give his name to a short but violent confrontation with white settlers — The Black Hawk War of 1832.

Ma-ka-tai-me-she-kia-ki-ak, the Indian spelling of his name, translated in English became Black Sparrow Hawk. He was a member of the combined Sac and Fox Indian Nation, supporter of the British and aide-de-camp to the great Indian Chief Tecumseh.

Black Hawk, although never a tribal chief, was a leader of the young braves of the tribe. His hatred of the U.S. government and its citizens was manifested in his disavowal of two 1804 treaties negotiated by William Henry Harrison. The Indian leader fought on the side of the British in the War of 1812 when he and his warriors were known as "Black Hawk's Band."

The war chief's effort to enlist assistance from the various Indian tribes to drive the white settlers from lands he claimed belonged to his people led to a long series of battles and skirmishes finally culminating in the Black Hawk War.

On May 8, 1832, the Illinois militia including a 23-year-old Abraham Lincoln arrived at Dixon's Ferry to be sworn into Army service by General Henry Atkinson. Shortly before the militia had arrived "Father" John Dixon had been visited by Black Hawk and some of his war chiefs who had set up camp north of the Rock River ferry operated by Dixon.

Black Hawk and Dixon had become acquainted at an earlier date and although Dixon tried to stop the war chief's band from continuing their aggression against the white man, they parted friends in this, the last time they were to meet.

ALTHOUGH MOST OF THESE NOTABLE FIGURES GAINED NATIONAL STATUS DURING AND AFTER THE CIVIL WAR, THEIR EARLY CAREERS FOUND THEM STATIONED AT FORT DIXON DURING THE BLACK HAWK WAR:

GENERAL WINFIELD SCOTT

GENERAL ZACHARY TAYLOR

ROBERT ANDERSON

JEFFERSON DAVIS

GENERAL W.S. HARNEY

GENERAL ALBERT JOHNSTON

No contemporary picture of Fort Dixon has ever been uncovered. However, Noah Brooks, a friend of Abraham Lincoln, lived and worked in Dixon and painted a picture of the old fort with its four-foot high embankments of sod surrounding it.

The two blockhouses were constructed of logs; one being four times larger than the other and provided with gunports on two sides, the smaller log structure was probably a powder magazine.

Many men who would later gain lasting places in history served in the United States Army at Fort Dixon during the Black Hawk War of 1832.

It was here, across the Rock River from "Father" John Dixon's home and business, that Captain Abe Lincoln saw the only active military service of his life. Lincoln had been mustered into Federal service at Rock Island after having been elected captain of a group of Sangamon County volunteers on April 21, 1832. His command, a company of 1,500 militia, arrived at Fort Dixon on May 15, 1832.

Lincoln served 2½ months in Army service; a total of 18 days of it in or near Fort Dixon. Although he often made light of his military experience, of his election as Captain he wrote, in 1859: "This was a success which gave me more pleasure than any I have had since."

FORT DIXON

DANIEL W. MCKENNEY

The horse was this country's major source of transportation creature for many years and every early settlement made arrangements to accommodate them. A livery's function was supplying horses and rigs to salesmen, doctors, professional men and suitors seeking to impress their young ladies. Horses and proper equipment were greatly in demand for such events as weddings, parties, picnics and funerals. The livery stable was also the gathering place for town loafers to gossip and tell the latest tall story or off-color joke.

The D.W. McKenney and Company Livery was for many years located on Water (River) Street west of the Galena Avenue bridge. The two-story section of the complex was built in 1841 by J.T. Little to house the Little and Brooks Dry Goods Store and later, a store owned by Webb, Rogers and Woodruff. In second floor rooms of the building were located offices of the *Dixon Telegraph* and *Lee County Herald* where the community's first newspaper was published on May 1, 1851.

Daniel W. McKenney, shown holding the horse on the right in the picture was born in Canada. He came to Dixon in 1848 at the age of 18 and became prosperous and well known in the community over the passing years.

McKenney constructed the flat-roof building pictured and later joined it to the original structure. The lean-to stable at the twin building's left was added later.

JOHN DEMENT

Colonel John Dement, statesman, soldier, industrialist, banker and community-minded Dixonite for over a half century, was born April 26, 1804 in Gallatin, Tennessee. When he was 13, he moved with his parents to Franklin County, Illinois, where he lived until he was 21.

At that young age, Dement was elected Sheriff of Franklin County; the youngest man ever elevated to that post in the southern Illinois county. In 1828, Dement was elected to the Illinois House of Representatives for two terms and, later, served three successive terms as Treasurer of the State of Illinois.

In 1836, after service as a Colonel in the Black Hawk War of 1832, Dement began another long series of elected positions in Illinois including State Representative, Receiver at the Federal Land Office, Presidential Elector in 1844 and member of the State Constitutional Convention in 1848, 1862, and 1870.

Colonel Dement's state-wide political activity never overshadowed his long, local interest in the growth and expansion of Dixon. In 1846 and 1851, he served on the Board of Directors of the Rock River Dam and Bridge Company, started the Dixon Plow Works in 1856, the Dixon Flax Bagging Mill in 1865, founded the Shabbona/Dement House in 1868 and was an organizer of the Dixon National Bank when it was founded, serving as that institution's first vice-president in 1871.

From its first beginnings, the western business district of Dixon has been named in Colonel Dement's honor with an additional tribute paid him in 1891 when Washington Street was renamed Dement Avenue in his memory. Colonel Dement, Dixon's mayor for four consecutive terms, died at his West First Street home in 1883.

JOHN EUSTACE

John V. Eustace is pictured in a formal pose for a portrait photographer in 1863. Eustace arrived in Dixon in 1843 at the age of 22 from his home in Pennsylvania. He was Superintendent of Schools in Dixon from 1850 to 1853 and a Director of the Dixon Dam and Bridge Company beginning in 1851. In that same year, John Eustace began the practice of law with his partner S.G. Patrick and in 1852, built the home later owned by James Charters overlooking the Rock River at North Brinton Avenue and East Boyd Street. He owned the *Dixon Evening Telegraph* from 1852 to 1854 and served as a Provost Marshal during the Civil War. In March, 1855, he was elected a Dixon town trustee and later served two terms as a Representative in the Illinois House. Together with E.B. Stiles and I.W. Atherton he purchased the *Dixon Monitor* newspaper after it had failed, changing its name to the *Dixon Advertiser*. In 1876, Eustace was a candidate for the position of Illinois Attorney General and in 1877, was elected Judge of the Lee County Circuit Court where he served for eight years before retiring from the bench in 1884.

JOSEPH CRAWFORD

Joseph Crawford arrived in the Dixon area in May, 1835, after having lived in Columbia, Pennsylvania since his birth in 1811. He first settled and farmed on land in the bend area between Lost Nation and Grand Detour along the Rock River. Four years after his arrival, Crawford was elected a member of the first Lee County Board of Supervisors and was elected County Surveyor, a position he held for 18 years. Crawford platted the original survey of Dixon in 1840 and made most of the surveys for the villages on the Rock River between Rockford and Rock Island. He was appointed acting mayor of Dixon in 1849 and was elected Mayor for three terms following that date. In addition, he was a member of the Illinois Legislature from 1849 to 1853 and a long time Trustee of the Northern Illinois Normal School in Dixon. In January, 1865, Crawford became President of the Lee County National Bank, a position he held until the time of his death in 1891 at the age of 80.

DR. OLIVER EVERETT

Born in Worthington, Massachusetts, September 12, 1811, Oliver Everett was one of a family of 15 children. He graduated from Berkshire Medical College. At the age of 25, he traveled from the East to Illinois intending to settle in Princeton where relatives resided. Upon reaching Chicago, he found no transportation was available so he walked the 105 miles carrying a suitcase of clothes and a chest of medical instruments and medicines. In 1836, he purchased a horse and rode north to Dixon's Ferry where he decided to settle. For the next 52 years Dr. Everett practiced medicine in and about Dixon and became one of the leading citizens of the growing community. Not only Dixon's but Lee County's pioneer doctor and in his time one of the best loved and most respected men in the state, Dr. Everett's nationally known reputation as a geologist and naturalist placed his name in high medical and academic circles across the land. Some of his collections, gathered from youth to old age, are on display at Dixon's Loveland Community House. In 1862, Dr. Everett went south to assist Federal armies at the Battle of Shiloh and the following year, he was elected Mayor of Dixon. In 1886, the fiftieth anniversary of his arrival in Dixon was celebrated throughout the city. Following a short illness, Dr. Oliver Everett died in Dixon on May 1, 1888, at the age of 77.

ELIAS B. STILES
Elias B. Stiles strikes an elegant pose for the camera in this formal photograph. Stiles, a native of Pennsylvania, came to Dixon in 1840 and became very active in community affairs. He was Lee County Treasurer from 1850 to 1857, a private banker, one of three men who built the Exchange Block in 1854 and at different times, owned both the Nachusa House and the *Dixon Advertiser*. At the time of his death on September 1, 1881, he was a Chicago grain dealer and broker as well as a market speculator.

JAMES K. EDSALL
Born in Windham, New York in 1831, James K. Edsall first came to Dixon during the 1856 presidential campaign of Colonel John C. Fremont. At the time, he was a member of the Kansas Legislature and active in state affairs. Due to the politics of the time, which he felt limited his freedom, he resettled in Dixon for the remainder of his life. He was appointed City Attorney in 1857 and became Mayor of Dixon in 1864. Edsall served as Illinois State Senator from 1870 to 1872 and as Secretary of State from 1873 to 1881. He died in Dixon on June 19, 1892.

SAMUEL M. BOWMAN
Samuel M. Bowman, who arrived in Dixon in 1837, holds the distinction of being the first retail merchant in Dixon after "Father" John Dixon. A native of Pennsylvania, Bowman was also the contractor for the Lee County Courthouse in 1840 and, with his partner, Charles Lane, platted the original town of Dixon in the same year. He was a member of the first Methodist Church congregation and also a trustee of that church. He left Dixon in the late 1840's to become a distinguished lawyer in San Francisco, Baltimore and Kansas City. Bowman was a Major General during the Civil War. A life long friend of General William T. Sherman, Bowman was the Civil War General's chosen biographer.

NOAH BROOKS
Noah Brooks operated a furniture business on South Galena Avenue next door to the Alexander and Howell Hardware Company for many years. He was an author and accomplished artist having drawn, at "Father" John Dixon's dictation, pictures of the original Dixon log cabin home and Fort Dixon. A personal friend of Abraham Lincoln, Brooks left Dixon in 1862 for California and later, became a Washington newspaper correspondent.

DIXON TELEGRAPH

Dixon's first newspaper has been published continuously since the initial issue of the *Dixon Telegraph* and *Lee County Herald* was printed on May 1, 1851. The newspaper's founder was Charles B. Fish, a printer and retired Presbyterian minister, who arrived in Dixon by horse drawn wagon carrying a Washington Hand Press, some ink, and a few rolls of newsprint over 136 years ago.

The 1837 creation of the telegraph by Samuel B. Morse gave the Dixon newspaper its name. In addition to the receipt of news, mail service and eye-witness reports, the telegraph also furnished the Dixon newspapers with a constant supply of useful information to present to its readers.

Editor Fish hired Benjamin F. Shaw, then 20, as publisher of his infant newspaper. A short 5½ months later the editor sold the newspaper to F. Hooper and M.P. Bull who changed the paper's name to the *Telegraph and Herald*. Another name change came on December 3, 1851, when the paper assumed the title of the *Dixon Telegraph* and Hopper withdrew from the ownership of the paper.

M.P. Bull ran the local paper until the end of January, 1852, when John V. Eustace purchased his interests in the enterprise. Eustace became editor and proprietor of the paper with B.F. Shaw continuing as publisher.

The *Dixon Evening Telegraph* was published as a weekly until 1887 when it became a daily paper. The publication has been printed in eleven different locations in the community since its first office above a dry goods store on River Street in 1851.

The publication moved into its current facility in 1959 and in 1986 underwent yet another name switch that saw its banner changed from the *Dixon Evening Telegraph* to the *Dixon Telegraph*.

BENJAMIN F. SHAW

Benjamin Flower Shaw was born March 31, 1831, in Waverly, New York. In his teens, he traveled west to join his brother Alonzo in Tipton, Iowa. When 14, young Shaw was hired to ride a 100 mile pony express mail route between Cedar Rapids, Iowa and Galena in northwestern Illinois.

In 1847, he moved to Rock Island, Illinois, where he entered the printing trade. When 20 years old, B.F. Shaw moved to the village of Dixon where he became the publisher of the new *Dixon Telegraph* and *Lee County Herald* then owned by Charles B. Fisk.

On May 1, 1851, the initial issue of that paper, which has been printed continuously ever since, carried this message from its young publisher:

> *Independent in politics and religion, we shall show respect to all parties and endeavors so far as we may in consistence with our position, to do justice to all.*

B.F. Shaw, in 1856, was one of the founders of the Illinois Republican party and a great supporter of its first presidential candidate, Colonel John C. Fremont. When gold was discovered in 1859 at Pike's Peak, Shaw left his newspaper position to travel west in search of a large fortune.

Shaw's Colorado efforts came to naught and he soon returned to Illinois to become publisher of the *Amboy Times* newspaper. He was later to serve two terms (1860 - 1868) as Circuit Clerk of Lee County and in 1868, went to Washington, D.C. as correspondent for the *Chicago Evening Journal*. The next year, Shaw was appointed by the Governor of Illinois to locate an asylum for the insane at Elgin. In 1870, he would return to Dixon to become associated with A.C. Bardwell as Editor of the *Dixon Telegraph and Herald*.

B.F. Shaw became Dixon's postmaster in 1891, a post he would hold with the exception of one four year term for the next 18 years. He was active in the planning of the community's new $60,000 Galena Avenue Post Office that was dedicated in 1911, two years after Shaw's death on September 18, 1909, at the age of 78.

Samuel Charters, in 1837, built this log cabin home situated on 640 acres of woodland forest on the west bank of the Rock River north of Dixon. The next year Samuel's brother, Alexander, came to reside in the cabin on the new estate he named Hazelwood.

Alexander Charters, born in Ireland in 1817, constructed a large home on his estate and became known over the years for his pleasant personality and warm hospitality. The honorary title of "Governor" was given Charters by those who came to be his friends. Of the "Governor," an early author noted: "On account of his handsome and commanding appearance, his elegant manners and his unrivaled hospitality he became known near and far."

Many visitors of fame and note stayed at Hazelwood in the early years. Abraham Lincoln, Stephen A. Douglas, William Cullen Bryant, Margaret Fuller and the like enjoyed the Charters' estate on the banks of the Rock River.

"Governor" Charters died September 18, 1878, at the age of 78 at his Hazelwood mansion.

GODFREY HOUSE

Located at 303 East Everett Street, this fine home was constructed in 1855 by J.B. Brooks, a pioneer Dixon businessman. Called the Godfrey House in honor of its second owner, William H. Godfrey owner in the 1860's of the Western Knitting Mills, the home was later purchased and remodeled by Dr. E.S. Murphy. The northside Dixon home is today the residence of Mrs. David L. Murphy.

DE PUY HOUSE

The home pictured is considered to be Dixon's oldest house. Located at 608 North Jefferson Avenue, it was built in 1837 by Reverend James De Puy (or De Pui) an Episcopal minister. Its first location was at the corner of East Everett Street and Jefferson Avenue, its second across the street and in the 1880's it was moved to its current site. "Father" John Dixon had offered De Puy his choice of North Dixon buildings lots if he would settle in Dixon. The minister accepted and lived in the community for many years. The original section of the home is made of hand-hewn logs with a frame cover.

THADDEUS D. BOARDMAN

This small brick house (above) with its double chimneys and white picket fence stood for years on West First Street between Highland and Madison Avenues. The home was the second owned by James P. Dixon, eldest son of "Father" John and Rebecca Dixon; the first being a small log cabin that also served as Dixon's first post office. In this home, Rebecca Dixon died in 1847. The house was located across the street from Colonel John Dement's large house and stood for many decades until its deteriorating condition caused it to be demolished.

A pioneer Dixon merchant, Thaddeus D. Boardman was born in New York in 1812 and came to Dixon in 1839. He was a member of the initial congregation of the Methodist Church and served many years as Secretary of the Sunday School beginning in 1843. Boardman owned and operated a thriving grist mill business in Grand Detour where he produced flour to sell in his retail Dixon store and through commission merchants throughout the mid-west. His home (shown below), built in 1851, was located at the corner of East Everett Street and North Dement Avenue.

JAMES P. DIXON

LEE COUNTY COURTHOUSE

Even before the formation of Lee County, efforts were being made to have Dixon's Ferry named as the county seat of Ogle County. Organized in 1836, Ogle County included territory now occupied by Lee County.

At the time of the first term of the Ogle County Circuit Court, there was no official courthouse building so court was convened in October, 1837, in the John Wilson blacksmith shop near John Dixon's home and business. In the following year, officials of the court ordered sessions to be held in the John Phelps home in Oregon.

The year 1839 saw the formation of Lee County with commissioners appointed by the Illinois Legislature designating Dixon as the county seat. The commissioners, D.G. Salsbury, H.H. Nichols and C.G. Butler, began the search for a proper building site for a formal courthouse structure.

"Father" John Dixon, after having been instrumental in both the formation of Lee County and the selection of Dixon as the county seat town, deeded to the new county the block square parcel of land on which to build the courthouse.

Numerous public minded Dixon citizens also secured bonds for money with which to build the structure. John Dixon also donated 80 acres of farmland to be sold at auction to raise money for the new edifice.

Samuel M. Bowman was the low bidder for the project with an original bid of $6,800. It was decided to use brick construction which added $810 to the bid price.

The first Lee County jail was also built in 1840 at a cost of $1,495. It was a hewed-log building built on a stone foundation at the northwest corner of Third Street and Ottawa Avenue.

This jail was to serve Lee County for 32 years until it was replaced in 1872. Prior to that time, however, the building served as headquarters for elected sheriffs of Lee County and the temporary home of hundreds of overnight guests and imprisoned persons.

Until the 1840 courthouse (top photo opposite page) was completed, terms of the Circuit Court were held in the original Dixon schoolhouse built in 1837. The largest room in the wooden building was 20 by 34 feet, more than large enough to handle the sessions of the early court.

Following the Civil War, the 1840 courthouse was found to be too small for the rapidly growing county. Citizens of Dixon with some assistance from the townships of Dixon, Palmyra and Nelson enlarged and remodeled the building (bottom photo opposite page). It was increased in size, the capacity of the court room doubled and several downstairs rooms were added. A new cupola was placed on the roof, a large Grecian porch with full length columns added to the front and many interior improvements made. Zachariah Luckey, the builder of the 1859 Luckey Bridge over the Rock River, served as architect for the project.

In 1870, a vault extension was erected to the east of the main building to hold court records and real estate transfers. This addition cost $3,033.75 to build and was the last major improvement made to the building before it was replaced by the current Lee County Court House in 1900.

"Father" Dixon had the foresight to see the advantages of making Dixon the county seat of Lee County and, as he did in other activities, "put his money (and land) where his mouth was" in order to secure its location in his home community.

CIRCUIT COURT

The Circuit Court, in session when this early photograph was made, was the law and justice center of Lee County. It was the meetingplace for Stephen A. Douglas when he eloquently advocated the election of Franklin Pierce and also for Lyman Trumbull, John A. Logan, Hon. E.B. Washburne and Thomas Campbell of Galena together with a host of other celebrities over the years. The voices of eminent lawyers and jurists, both of national and local fame, were heard within its walls. The 1855 life-size portrait of "Father" John Dixon by Ferris Finch can be seen on the wall behind the seated judge.

EARLY HOTELS

This early view of Galena Avenue looking north across the Rock River shows the second location of the City Hotel. On the right, the hotel's sign can be seen beneath the "Oysters" advertising sign.

The Nachusa House, opened in 1853, has continually operated ever since.

Hotels in Dixon have been prosperous and numerous as the community expanded. "Father" John Dixon's log cabin home, where overnight guests often slept on the crude wood floor, was the community's first.

In the winter of 1836-37 Peter McKinney and H. Thompson started the Western Hotel which later became the Huntley House. The Rock River House at the corner of Galena and River Streets later (in 1837) was renamed the Phoenix Hotel. It was destroyed by fire in 1846.

In 1840, the Dixon House was built on West First Street. Twelve years later, it was moved by owner Henry McKenney to Galena Avenue where it became known as the City Hotel. The Nachusa House, begun as the Dixon Hotel Company in 1835, was slow to be constructed but finally opened after years of delay in 1853. The Washington House, a large brick hotel building in downtown Dixon opened in October, 1854, followed three years later by the Shabbona/Dement House in Dementtown. It underwent a name change in 1868 becoming the St. James Hotel and finally burned to the ground in 1871.

Dementtown had another hotel, the Waverly House, opened in April, 1860. It was built to serve the large railroad business then active in that section of Dixon. Later, the Transient House was also to locate in Dixon's western section.

1866 saw the new Keystone House on West First Street open to the public in a large three-story downtown brick building near the southwest corner of Galena Avenue. In 1880, a large hotel/boardinghouse was located on Hennepin Avenue calling itself the Revere House.

Through the years, other hotels of one size or another have serviced the needs of Dixon's visitors and transients. Only one of the early hotels still exists - the famous Nachusa House.

The Shabbona/Dement House opened October, 1857. It later became the St. James Hotel and burned on November, 1871.

The Waverly House, located along the railroad tracks in Dementtown, opened April, 1860 and was demolished late in the 1890's.

The Transient House was another hotel built to serve the needs of railroad workers and passengers. It opened in the late 1880's.

The Washington House began business in October, 1854, and served the Dixon area community until demolished in the late 1970's.

The Dixon Plow Works was established by Colonel John Dement a short five years before the Civil War and 20 years after John Deere and Major Leonard Andrus had established the Grand Detour Plow Works.

The first location of Dement's plow making machine shop was said to have been on West Third Street near Peoria Avenue. The factory was soon moved to two buildings on East River Street where an improved plow was turned out using a special hardened steel. In full operation 75 men were employed who produced up to 30 finished plows per day.

On July 16, 1857, two local men, Brooks and Daily, purchased the machine shop owned by Dement's Plow Works and converted the rock building into a flour mill operation. Ten years later, in 1867, Colonel Dement sold his growing firm to his son, Henry D. Dement and W.M. Todd. The plow works then produced products to be sold almost exclusively to the F.K. Orvis Company of Chicago.

Franklin K. Orvis, who had come to Chicago from Vermont, moved to Dixon in 1869. That same year he purchased the entire Dixon Plow Works operation. The company was later organized as the Orvis Manufacturing Company and was sold to Charles W. Curtis, Chicago, in 1879.

Next called the Orvis Plow Company (in 1880), the firm was managed by F.K. Orvis' brother, John. In the April, 1880, fire that destroyed the Becker and Underwood Flouring Mills and several other factories in the same East River Street area, the Curtis Plow Works received a great deal of damage and with no insurance available to cover the loss, went out of business soon thereafter.

DIXON PLOW WORKS

STREET ARCHES

THIRD STREET

WEST FIRST STREET

The Galena Limestone arches spanning First, Second and Third Streets between Monroe and College Avenues in Dixon's southwest area, are the handiwork of Robert F. Laing. The railroad arches were finished and in place when the first steam locomotives arrived in Dixon in February, 1855.

Laing, a native of Edinburgh, Scotland, became a contractor for the Illinois Central Railroad when he arrived in Illinois in 1851. His job was to both build the five massive piers for the 1,056-foot railroad bridge that reached 56-feet above the Rock River at Dixon as well as the three stone arches still in place today.

The stone mason so liked Dixon that he sent for his wife and children and established a home on East Everett Street where he resided for the rest of his life. A model of his railroad bridge piers can still be seen in the Loveland Community House Museum.

The stone used in the piers and arches was called Galena Limestone, able to support great weights and withhold tremendous pressure from ice and debris during the time of spring river floods. All the stone was quarried from the Dement Quarry on Dixon's northeast side along the Rock River.

The three street arches, due to the contour of the land, are of different heights. The Second Street arch has a 15-foot clearance, the First Street arch 14-feet and the "Little Sister" arch over Third Street has a 12-foot clearance. The large limestones were so perfectly cut, shaped and balanced that they have withstood the vicissitudes of time without a noticeable shift or crack.

The first Illinois Central Railroad Bridge in Dixon was laid on top of the five stone piers standing in the Rock River. The wooden bridge structure was completed early in 1855. It was replaced in 1862 with an all-iron bridge that lasted 55 years before being replaced by the current railroad bridge and massive cement piers.

The three stone arches continue even yet today to stand strong and proud after over 135 years of continuing service to the community of Dixon.

SECOND STREET

Abraham Lincoln, 16th President of the United States, was born February 12, 1809, in Hardin County, Kentucky. When he traveled to Dixon in July, 1856, to deliver one of over 50 speeches he would make that summer on behalf of Colonel John C. Fremont, first Republican Party candidate for President, he was 47 years old.

This was one of the few times he had returned to Dixon since his military service in the Black Hawk War of 1832. The *Amboy Times*, in describing Lincoln in his Dixon appearance, wrote:

> "— a man with slow and dignified motion, but quick as a flash and, lo, what a man! He is about 6 feet high, crock-legged, stoop-shouldered, spare built and anything but handsome in the face."

In 1903, a large granite marker was placed on the east lawn of the Lee County Courthouse to commemorate Lincoln's Dixon speech.

LINCOLN SPEECH

PORTRAIT OF JOHN DIXON

A large, life-size, oil portrait of the founder and namesake of the community, "Father" John Dixon, was painted from life by Ferris Finch.

Dixon, at the time, was 70 years old having arrived in Dixon in 1830 at the age of 46. He would live another 21 years after the painting was completed in 1855.

Finch was a struggling young artist at the time traveling west in search of fame and fortune when he stopped in Dixon. Making the acquaintance of several local people, the youthful painter decided to remain in the little riverside community for a time.

At the suggestion of several people, the local newspaper organized a subscription fund to hire Finch to paint a life-size portrait of "Father" Dixon.

Upon completion of the portrait, Dixon and Finch unveiled it at a public display late in 1855. After several months, the portrait was hung in the 1840 Lee County Court House. The portrait remained in that building until after the turn-of-the-century when it was stored awaiting the construction of the current courthouse in 1901.

Of late the portrait has been removed from the Lee County building and has been on public display in Dixon's Loveland Community House.

CHOLERA EPIDEMIC

> "Death in its most frightful form swept our heretofore healthy town like an avalanche, carrying away within the space of 24 hours, 19 souls."

So began an accounting of the July-August, 1854, Dixon cholera epidemic in the *Telegraph* and *Herald* newspaper. The little community at the time had no hospital and the services of only two doctors both of whom worked night and day to assist the local population in their great time of need.

Drs. Everett and Abbott were treating the spreading disease with a combination of powdered charcoal and whisky. The newspaper suggested to its readers that they "shake an ounce of whisky until it foams and drink this three times a week and avoid all excesses." Results were not guaranteed.

Early in August, 1854, the epidemic reached its height. A large plot of ground in Oakwood Cemetery was readied for the victims of the disease. A series of deep trenches were dug and the remains of the dead placed in these hurried mass graves, covered with lime and earth and left unmarked.

A total of 34 Dixonites died in the cholera epidemic of 1854. How many others died during this time from the same cause and were treated elsewhere by other medical personages is not known. Nor, for that matter, is anything known of those who may have passed away from the illness and were buried without formal notice to local authorities.

The summer of 1854 remains in local history as the most dreadful of any since that time. As the newspaper of the day noted with sadness, "Ah, how truly it is that in the midst of life we are in death."

This distinguished group of early Dixon men posed for the photographer in a rather somber mood. Standing, left to right, are: Albert Ferguson, J.H. Moore and Frederick Truman. Seated are: Joseph T. Little, Reverend J.H. Pratt and Eli C. Smith.

CHAPTER II

EXPANSION YEARS

1860 - 1889

As the first half of the 19th century neared its conclusion, Dixon stood at the brink of great industrial prosperity. In the 30 years since its founding, the city on the Rock River had attracted a good selection of industrial concerns due to its available waterpower, central location, excellent employee base and growth potential.

Dixon's major industries in 1860 consisted of the Roberts and McKay Hat and Cap Factory, the R. P. Robinson Corn Mill, the Platt and Son Harrow Plant and the Leather Manufactory owned by local entrepreneurs Morse and Benjamin. The flour mills created by Brooks and Dement and by Charles Godfrey together with Colonel Dement's Dixon Plow Works and the local Woolen Mill gave steady employment to local workers. These industrial activities helped spread Dixon's name as a progressive city across the nation.

The local business district maintained an expansionist attitude although a March 7, 1861 fire caused considerable damage to buildings near the corner of Main Street and Galena Avenue. Businessmen of the city were instrumental in the formation of the Dixon Improvement Association; a group "formed for the purpose of improving and beautifying the city by planting trees, etc."

The newest bridge was opened across the Rock River on the first of January, 1861, after a New Year's Eve "Free Bridge Party" celebrated the event at the Nachusa House.

Business improved with the completion of the Free Bridge. People, vehicles and livestock were able to move back and forth across the Rock River with ease. For a time, considerable interest in promoting the near north side of the Rock River as an industrial site was shown. It wasn't until 1870, however, that a factory was established along the north shore of the river. The Northwestern Wind Mill Works owned by Thomas C. Little and Company was to be the single major industry so located.

All things considered, Dixon wore a cheerful face in spite of the gloomy news coming from the south and east concerning the activities of the southern states of the Union.

A decided northern sympathy existed in Dixon at the time. So much so that when the first shots were fired by Confederate forces on Federal soldiers stationed at Fort Sumter off Charleston, South Carolina, a company of Dixon volunteers was immediately formed.

On April 21, 1861, the first Dixon company of volunteers headed by Captain A.B. Gorgas was organized. A flag was flown across from the Mayor's office bearing the motto *THE UNION FOREVER* and all in the small community pledged their support of Mr. Lincoln's government.

Young boys of the town were patriotic in forming a club to "do chores" and in other ways assist soldiers, widows and their families. The women and girls of Dixon sewed uniforms and made bandages for those serving in the Army while all hoped and prayed the terrible fighting would soon end. As each Union victory was reported celebrations were held to honor the brave men and boys involved. When groups were mustered out of military service joyous welcome home celebrations were conducted.

By April 9, 1865, when General U.S. Grant received the surrender of General Robert E. Lee at Appomattox Court House, Virginia, over 2,454 young boys and men had left Dixon for military service. With the end of the fighting, the troops returned home --- heroes all --- and once again took up the peaceful pursuits of civilian life.

In 1862, the Illinois Central Railroad Company built an iron bridge, in place of the wooden truss work, on the original limestone piers without stopping a single train crossing over the Rock River. The following year repairs by John H. Cropsey to the mill-dam upstream cost over $10,000 and added greatly to the industrial picture of Dixon.

Manufacturing operations after the Civil War that produced plows, wood products, woolen cloth and flour all recovered rapidly from any post-war depression that they may have felt. Colonel Dement's Flax Bagging Mill, operated by Jerome and Downing, was a direct result of favorable conditions existing in Dixon following the end of the War Between The States.

Western expansion after the war took off with great strides. The National Homestead Act allowed thousands of veterans the opportunity for a new life with the gift of 160 acres of free government land. Dixon's central location in northern Illinois served as a starting place for departing families going west.

The fall of 1868 marked the end of one era and the beginning of another when Theron Cumins and Henry T. Noble announced plans to move the Grand Detour Plow Works from that village to Dixon. Begun in 1837 by John Deere and Major Leonard Andrus, the Grand Detour Plow Works was the most important factory in the village six miles upstream on the Rock River from Dixon. Its removal to Dixon marked the start of a gradual decline in Grand Detour's fortunes and the start of a long and profitable plow making endeavor in Dixon.

All through the rest of the late 1800's, grade and high school buildings were constructed. The Red Brick, White Brick and North Dixon High Schools were built, and the Rock River Military Academy and Steinman Institute soon became a part of the local educational scene. Too, the Rock River University continued to be an important part of Dixon life. The 1881 debut of Dixon College served notice on the community that higher educational endeavors were a well established fact of life. In 1897, classes of St. Mary's School were begun in a fine frame building on the city's south side.

For public school purposes, Dixon was divided into two school districts. In the winter of 1868-69, the north side district erected a $20,000 school building at the very edge of the northern part of the city; the location today of Heritage Square. The facility was topped with a mansard roof crowned by a belfry. At the time the school was opened, 180 pupils were in attendance with C.O. Scudder serving as Principal. The South Side School District, in the summer of 1869, built a $32,000 brick structure that was the most imposing building in the erea. There were 459 pupils enrolled under the direction of Superintendent E.C. Smith.

When the Truesdell iron bridge at the foot of Galena Avenue was dedicated in 1869, many Dixonites thought the structure would last well into the next century. On Sunday, May 4, 1873, however, the Truesdell Bridge collapsed into the Rock River, killing or injuring over 85 men, women and children gathered to witness a baptismal ceremony taking place just below the bridge.

The carriage and buggy works of Vann and Means produced an above average product, beginning in 1870 in a factory located on West Third Street. Likewise, the products of the Victor Scale Works, that existed from 1867 to 1870, bore the Dixon name with pride.

Until 1870, local fires had been fought by well-intended but under-equipped and untrained citizens. In that year, the Dixon Hose Company Number One was organized with about 30 members. Henry S. Dey was elected foreman. At the same time, the Monitor Hook and Ladder Company was brought together with W.N. Johnson chosen as their first foreman.

The building of Dixon's first City Hall, erected for the primary use of the fire department, became a prideful segment of city life after January, 1871. During this time Dixon's first formal lending library was established; the forerunner of the Dixon Public Library.

September 15, 1871, saw the establishment of the Dixon National Bank in facilities located mid-way in the Exchange Block on Galena Avenue. The first officers and directors of the financial institution were H.B. Jenks, H.S. Lucas, John Dement, Quartus Ely and James B. Charters. Jenks was chosen President, Ely Vice President and Lucas was elected Cashier.

A foursome of public utility services were made available to Dixon residents in the last part of the 19th century. Each would come to be accepted parts of every-day life in the community. They were:

— *WATER.* The 1871-72 laying of the first water mains from a rotary pump at the river's edge to the corner of Main Street and Galena Avenue was a greatly needed civic improvement. The $600 cost, considered high those many years ago, was the first of many such projects over the years in Dixon.

— *GAS.* The soft glow of gas lighting became a reality in Dixon on December 22, 1874, when the Western Excelsior Gas Company, followed by the Dixon Gas Lighting Company in 1877, began service to the community. Gas streetlamps and retail store gas lighting systems were the first uses made of the early utility. Later, homes and business places were furnished with lighting.

— *TELEPHONE.* The Central Telephone Company began in Dixon on July 14, 1881, when 44 telephones were put into operation. Miss Leona Mead was the day operator and John Mattox the night manager. The *Dixon Evening Telegraph* noted "The Telephone apparatus has arrived in our city. The lazy man's friend is here."

— *ELECTRICITY.* The initial electric plant in Dixon was installed in the Fletcher Planing Mill at the south end of the Rock River dam at the foot of Ottawa Avenue in 1882. Power from the mill was used to light the original dozen electric streetlamps in the downtown area of the city.

The office of Jason C. Ayers was the location, on November 25, 1872, for the first meeting of the local Young Men's Christian Association. At first, the Dixon Y, with 23 original members, leased rooms in Tillson's Hall and later, over the G.O. Wendel Jewelry Store on Main Street. The organization's first full-time employee, Philip Bevis, conducted Y activities from 1890 to 1901 when initial serious efforts were made toward the construction of a YMCA building.

The Dixon Opera House opened in the fall of 1876 with a performance by the Payson English Opera Company. This structure was to serve as the cultural and entertainment center of the community for almost 45 years.

Fire continued to take its toll of downtown buildings and industrial factories. The Galena Avenue Exchange Block building suffered a great deal of destruction in 1878. The following year, J.C. Mead's downtown book store caught fire, the home of Theodore Moeller burned and the Main Street residence of E.B. Stiles also saw the ravages of fire.

Termed "the most disastrous fire that ever visited our city" by the local newspapers, the Becker and Underwood Flour Mills caught fire and were destroyed on April 8, 1880. Assisted by the Amboy Fire Department, the local firefighters contained the blaze but only after fire had caused the death of two Dixonites and caused almost $200,000 in damages.

The industrial and commercial picture of Dixon, at this time, looked bleak. So, too, did the overall economic condition of the city as a national depression caused great concern among all Dixonites. This condition lasted for over two years before an upward trend was once again felt in the city.

An interesting industry began in the community in 1882 with the arrival of the Dixon Button Factory. Employing 60 people (mostly "single girls from 15 to 25 years of age" according to the newspaper report of the time), the firm's factory was located on West First Street near Harrison Avenue. A vegetable ivory imported from South America was used to produce over 300 gross of finished buttons daily in 60 different carded varieties.

Dixon's button business was brought to the city as a result of a $15,000 capital stock pledge made by local civic leaders. This effort to solicit and encourage new places of employment resulted in the formation of the Local Improvement League.

The building of the Dixon Water Works in 1883, at a cost of over $80,000, gave great hope for a constant source of pure water for residential, commercial and industrial use. Two years later, the forerunner of the present City Bank in Dixon was established giving Dixon another conservative financial business to serve its needs.

An announcement appearing in the local newspaper early in 1889 caused over 300 applicants to apply for four new city postal delivery routes. Dixon, with a population of 5,000 at the time, would see the final choice for postal carriers influenced by whether an applicant was the sole support of a widowed mother. The four men who received the jobs were Thomas Hoban, W.P. Devine, Herbert A. Morrison and Louis B. Atkins. The four were Dixon's first mailmen, worked a seven day week and were paid $600 per year in salary.

In the 25 years since the end of the Civil War, Dixon had made great strides forward. Industrial, commercial, residential, educational, spiritual and population growth was evident at every turn. As Dixon looked forward to the 20th century, the community did so with obvious pride and enthusiasm.

One of Dixon's main business blocks down through the years has been the southeast corner of East Main (First) Street and Galena Avenue. For many years known as the Exchange Block, this picture shows a Chicago artist's version of the business block. Built by E.B. Stiles, J.V. Eustace and H. Webb in 1854, some of the stores and offices at that time were: Exchange Bank, E.B. Stiles (real estate), Van Epps and Ashley (dry goods), W.S. Garrison (saloon), Ferris Finch (portrait painter), W.W. Curtis (hardware), John V. Eustace (attorney), Charles Abbott (druggist) and Yarney and Gilman (general merchandise).

In the 1870, the wooden sidewalks and dirty, rutted Galena Avenue was still in evidence in front of Dixon's Exchange Block. Wooden awnings were in use, a large street lamp could be seen at the corner and a change of business places could be noted. Some of those occupying space in the Exchange Block at the time were: The Lee Country Cast Store ("the cheapest store"), A. Wood Union Store, W.E. Van Epps (dry goods) and Varney and Gilman Store.

After the turn-of-the-century, Galena Avenue was paved, sidewalks cemented, swings of heavy cloth were in use and automobiles out numbered the rapidly vanishing horse and buggy transportation. Some of the occupants of Dixon's Exchange Block as seen in this photograph were: City National Bank, The Shoe Store, Sterling's Pharmacy, Lew E. Edwards Book Store, and E.R. Curtis and E.L. Kling jewelers.

The northwest corner of West Main (First) Street and Galena Avenue has seen great changes over the years. In the mid part of the 1800's, the still unpaved streets carried horsedrawn traffic while pedestrians used wooden boardwalks. The awning was drawn on the corner building to protect the goods shown within its window while the "fresh food" store next to it advertised its "one price - cash" business policy. The current location of the Dixon National Bank building, the corner was always a busy one in Dixon's early days.

Near the turn-of-the-century, a two story brick building was built on the corner of West First Street and Galena Avenue, later to be the home of the O.H. Brown Dry Goods and Carpet Store. In this photograph, circa 1910, automobiles, streetcar tracks and overhead electric power lines and electric advertising signs were much in evidence. Paved streets and sidewalks made shopping easier as downtown Dixon took on a more orderly appearance.

In the Roaring Twenties, West First Street shows great improvement with not only the five-story Dixon National Bank building but the three-story Union Hall building, constructed in 1855 as a four-story structure, much in evidence. Across Galena Avenue, the "Round-Corner Building", the Ebinger Building, has been reduced from three to two stories and a highly decorative street light and post stands guard over downtown Dixon activities.

THE THIRTEENTH INFANTRY ILLINOIS VOLUNTEERS
REUNIONS

The Thirteenth Infantry Illinois Volunteers served from May, 1861, to June, 1864, in Federal service during the War Between The States. Originally 970 men and boys, the regiment was much smaller when mustered out of service; attrition rates were severe.

Small, almost committee sized, reunions were held by the veterans of the Thirteenth Volunteers beginning the year after the end of their service. The first full-blown, all veterans invited reunion was conducted June 3, 1868 in Dixon.

Headquarters for this get-together, with over 200 in attendance, was the Nachusa House Tavern with all meetings conducted across Galena Avenue in the Lee County Courthouse.

As the years went by, time took its constant toll of the members of the Civil War battle group. Called now "The Old Thirteenth," in deference to its aging members and the passing of time, a crowd of 130 attended the 25th Silver Anniversary Reunion on May 24, 1886.

The 50th Golden Reunion of the Old Thirteenth was planned for May 24, 1911. Although only a small handful of the living veterans attended the meeting, they were treated royally by Dixonites. They were given a free trolley ride to Sterling on the Interurban, received a free dinner at the People's Church, had a boat ride to Grand Detour where luncheon was served at the Colonial Inn and attended a vaudeville show at the Family Theatre in downtown Dixon.

The 60th and final reunion of the Old Thirteenth was conducted in Dixon in 1921 with 14 of the 122 known survivors of the Civil War regiment in attendance.

THE THIRTEENTH ILLINOIS INFANTRY

The first regiment in the United States to be mustered into Federal service for a three-year term of duty during the Civil War began their military service in Dixon. It was on May 9, 1861, shortly after President Abraham Lincoln's call for long-time volunteers that the Thirteenth Infantry Illinois Volunteers were formed.

The Thirteenth went into camp on what was then Fairgrounds Park, located just south of the present Oakwood Cemetery property. The volunteers were mainly from Dixon and Lee County but also included men from various areas of mid-western Illinois.

The Thirteenth, first organized with 970 men, stayed in Dixon until June 16, when they were then sent by train to Missouri for training. After this period, the Thirteenth became the first regiment of Northern troops to reach the Chickasaw Bayou Battlefield where they led an assault against Southern forces on December 29, 1862.

They then fought in the Battle of Jackson (Mississippi) and were in the armed assault on the Rebel fortifications at Vicksburg. The regiment later returned to Jackson and participated in the long seige there until their Southern stronghold fell.

The Thirteenth Illinois Volunteers also fought at Tuscumbia, Lookout Mountain in Tennessee, Missionary Ridge and at Ringford, Georgia, where over a third of the regiment was lost in action.

When the regiment's three-year term of service ended in June, 1864, with the volunteers being mustered out of Federal service, many of the soldiers joined other military groups. The

majority, however, returned to their homes and became, for all practical purposes, prime candidates for yearly reunions of the Thirteenth for the next 60 years.

JOHN K. ROBINSON

Robinson, born in Ohio in 1809, settled in Dixon in May, 1832. He holds the honor of being Dixon's first school teacher as he taught the children of "Father" John Dixon in his log cabin home in the winter of 1833-34.

SOUTH SIDE PUBLIC SCHOOL

Erected in 1868, the Red Brick School was located on West Seventh Street and was known as the most imposing building on the city's south side. Note the students posing for this photograph by standing on the roof of the cupola of the school.

FIRST HIGH SCHOOL

The First Methodist Church building was constructed in the summer of 1843 at 117 East Second Street, opposite the Lee County Courthouse. This building was used as the first high school in Dixon.

NORTH SIDE PUBLIC SCHOOL

Built at a cost of over $20,000, the North Side Public School served the community for decades. In the late 1920's, it counted among its students a young Ronald Reagan.

Known by all as the White Brick School, it was erected in 1887 for $5,500. Enlarged in 1892-93 at a cost of $17,000, the building would later burn and be replaced by the present South Central School.

SOUTH CENTRAL SCHOOL

E.C. SMITH

One of Dixon's best known early educators was E.C. Smith. Born in New York state in 1829, Smith traveled west, after receiving his college education, to spend a year teaching in the public school system of Geneva, Illinois. Following this teaching assignment, in 1852, Professor Smith became Superintendent of the Rock Island (Illinois) Seminary for three years. He arrived in Dixon in 1855 to assist in the organization of the Dixon Collegiate Institute. In 1861, E.C. Smith began a long term of employment in the Dixon school system by being appointed to head the South Side School. In 1886, Professor Smith was appointed principal of the North Side High School, a position he held until his retirement. Smith also served as Deacon and Superintendent of Sunday School of the Baptist Church for over 40 years. The South Side School, build in 1886, was named the E.C. Smith School in his honor. Professor Smith died in Dixon on September 17, 1889, after devoting his adult life to the betterment of the citizens of his adopted community.

The Dixon Collegiate Institute began in 1855 under the direction of Rev. W.W. Harsha using rented rooms in the basement of the Lutheran Church. In July of that year, the cornerstone of the school's large building, located high above the Rock River on Bluff Park in Dixon's east side, was laid.

Dixon citizens had endowed the higher education facility with $25,000 plus a gift of the grounds, property and equipment needed. The Dixon Institute operated as primarily a boy's school until 1861 when it became known as the Dixon Female Seminary under Rev. O.W. Cooley. A later name change to that of the Rock River University (1875) caused a resultant switch in the school's educational goals.

For the quarter century the school operated, several investors, owners, and managers tended to its needs. Finally, a decline in financial support caused the Bluff Park school to discontinue its educational endeavors.

The imposing five-story brick building that had stood as a silent sentinel over Dixon for 25 years was later demolished to make way for an area of fine homes.

DIXON COLLEGIATE INSTITUTE

STEINMANN INSTITUTE

In an era before state operated institutions of higher education, private schools that operated on a for-profit business basis were popular. One of several such places of advanced study was the Steinmann Institute.

Beginning in downtown Dixon, C.A. Steinmann's business school saw the construction of its own building in 1895. The school's campus was located along the Rock River north of Assembly Park in the general area of what is now Myrtle Avenue and Prescott Street.

Classes taught in the institute included instrumental music, art, physical culture, voice, modern languages and kindergarten normal. Also several business-related subjects were offered. Early advertisements of the Steinmann Institute stressed the school's desire to "turn out a well-rounded man or woman

educated to fit into the nature of the business world as it is accomplished at this time."

A dormitory was built for students in 1903. A Chautauqua Hall was also constructed for use not only by the institute but by citizens of the community as well.

A.H. Stoddad's Conservatory of Music made use of Steinmann Institute after that organization went out of business. Another educational endeavor, the Rock River Military Academy, took over use of the facilities after this time.

The Military Academy, a boy's boarding school with a heavy emphasis on military-like discipline and scholarship, was a fixture in Dixon for many years. The Boy's Dormitory, located on the property, was destroyed in a $10,000 fire in January, 1915. The Rock River Military Academy ceased to exist shortly thereafter.

DIXON COLLEGE

A 25-year-old Indiana educator and businessman, Professor J.B. Dille, arrived in Dixon following a cold winter snowfall in January, 1881. He was in Dixon, then a bustling city of 2,500 residents, to encourage local businessmen and civic leaders to begin a college. Dille met with Professor E.C. Smith, Colonel Henry T. Noble, W.B. Higgins and other leading Dixonites who later pledged $25,000 in scholarships to start the Northern Illinois Normal School and Dixon Business College.

Dille leased the large building and four acres of land that recently had been the home of various colleges and seminaries in Bluff Park for a three year period. He also published 10,000 copies of an 18 page circular promoting the new college and its staff. Dille's father-in-law, John C. Flint, was named President of the school with Dille acting as Principal and teacher along with seven other teachers all from his hometown of Valparaiso, Indiana.

Attendance was so great the first year that additional rooms in downtown Dixon were rented to serve as classrooms. In 1882, a pair of new three-story brick buildings were erected in west Dixon with a third building completed in 1888 to serve as a new dormitory.

From an initial enrollment of 52 students to over 2,000 in 1895 with a faculty of 30 men and women, the local college became known as the finest and best equipped in northern Illinois.

John C. Flint was both President of the Dixon College and its chief financial backer from 1881 to 1902 when he and Dille severed their business relationship. Flint died in 1907 and Dille in 1930 at the age of 74.

An estimated 40,000 men and women attended the school in its 33 years of existence. From 1898 to 1901, it was considered to be the largest law school in Illinois. Under the direction of Edward E. Wingert and James E. Watts, hundreds of graduates of the Dixon College Law Department went on to become lawyers, judges and high ranking holders of political office. In 1902, over 1,000 students enrolled for the fall semester; more than attended the University of Illinois in the same year. The school's colors, yellow and black, were familiar sights in Dixon and on the athletic fields of rival colleges.

From 1902 to 1912, the college had a series of owners until Lee County Superintendent of Schools, I. Frank Edwards of Amboy, purchased the institute. Edwards operated the college for just two years before finally closing it in 1914, 33 years after its founding. The school's buildings were sold for use as factories and its campus divided into residential buildings lots. The college's large athletic field was offered to the City of Dixon for use as a park but a public referendum turned down the idea.

Philip Maxwell Alexander — 1819 - 1898

George L. Howell — 1820 - 1893

ALEXANDER & HOWELL

When Philip M. Alexander first arrived at Dixon's Ferry in 1838 at the age of 19 he worked on "Father" John Dixon's farm for several months. He and Richard Loveland were then employed by Smith Gilbraith to cut timber for firewood on the large Rock River island later known as Van Arnam's Island. Firewood then sold for $1.25 per cord. Alexander later worked for J.T. Little and J.B. Brooks in their retail stores. In 1848, he went back East to marry Eliza Howell who later died in the 1873 Truesdell Bridge disaster. In 1853, he was elected as one of Dixon's first town trustees. The following year George L. Howell, Alexander's brother-in-law, arrived in Dixon with his wife and family to enter into a business partnership that would last until their deaths. The Alexander and Howell Hardware Company, located on South Galena Avenue from 1854 until the late 1970's, became one of Dixon's major retail business concerns. The firm was one of the first two such business enterprises in the entire state. After the death of Philip Alexander in 1898, owners of the business included Howell and Sullivan, E.N. Howell and from 1930 to 1976, Vernon and Gladys Massey.

The Howell Home — Constructed circa 1855

ALEXANDER HOME

One of Dixon's more imposing homes was built by Phillip M. Alexander. When completed in 1863-64, the Alexander home was considered one of the best examples of Greek Revival architecture in the community. The home was a copy of a similar structure Alexander and his wife, Eliza Howell Alexander, had admired in Utica, New York, prior to their arrival in Dixon in 1848. The original cost of the home was $6,669.23 with the bill of sale for the home containing these "extras": stairs to attic -$10; five marble mantels - $152; floor in attic - $50; plaster of paris cornice in parlor and main hall - $100.

The house was later owned by Alexander's daughter, Elizabeth Maude, and her husband, the son of Major Leonard Andrus. Colonel William B. Brinton purchased the house before the turn-of-the-century and in 1926 donated the large structure to the local Masonic organization for use as the Masonic Temple.

The Alexander and Howell Hardware Store, on the right, was next door to Camp and Son, furniture and undertaking, on South Galena Avenue.

CATHOLIC CHURCH

The 25 Catholic families who had been added to Dixon's population by 1854 were the original members of the church when St. Patrick's parish was organized in the community. At first services were held in the Lee County Courthouse lobby by Father James Fitzgerald until the first frame church was constructed on Highland Avenue between Fifth and Sixth Streets. Foundations for the present red brick Catholic church were laid in 1869. The cornerstone ceremonies were conducted on June 23, 1872 and regular services begun late in 1872.

The church suffered a great fire in 1887 but was rebuilt a year later at a cost of about $20,000 using the original exterior walls of the edifice which remained standing following the fire. In 1896, St. Patrick's church was called the finest between Chicago and Omaha in point of interior decoration. The ceiling was done in frescoed work with scenes from the life of Christ in full size. The walls were hung with elaborate paintings. Various carvings and the altar were said to have been magnificent works of art.

PRESBYTERIAN CHURCH

The First Presbyterian Church in Dixon began in 1851 with services being conducted in the village's small schoolhouse. There were originally ten members of the church who met with Dr. W.W. Harsha. The minister had come to Dixon to establish the Dixon Collegiate Institute and to serve as the leader of the local Presbyterian Church. Soon after the Collegiate Institute was opened, the First Presbyterian Church building was dedicated on February 17, 1856. On January 1, 1861, the Presbyterians moved to a building in North Dixon formerly occupied by the Unitarian Church while the Congregational Church moved into the former Presbyterian building. The present church was erected on East Third Street across from the Lee County Courthouse in 1863 at a cost of $5,000. Of dressed native limestone construction, the church featured a 130-foot bell tower containing a 2,000 pound bell.

BAPTIST CHURCH

A group of seven Baptists from the tiny community of Dixon's Ferry organized the First Baptist Church on May 28, 1838. A $3,000 structure was built as a church on East First Street near Ottawa Avenue in 1849 on a site purchased six years before for $100. The $3,000 necessary to build the church was raised by selling stock in the building to members of the congregation and by selling and assigning parishioners certain pews in the church. At this time the church had a membership of 44 and paid its minister, Rev. E.T. Manning, a salary of $300 per year in addition to his house rent and firewood. The present First Baptist Church saw cornerstone ceremonies conducted on October 1, 1869, and dedication services completed on July 28, 1872. The structure, located on East Second Street between Galena and Ottawa Avenues, cost $15,000. So well built was the 1872 church building that the rampaging fire of February, 1920, that destroyed the Opera House located on Galena Avenue, did little or no damage to the edifice although the two buildings were situated very close to each other.

METHODIST CHURCH

The first formal religious service held at Dixon's Ferry was conducted by L.A. Sugg, a young Methodist missionary in 1834. May 7, 1837 saw the first meeting of a Methodist congregation with seven members present. Meetings were first held on the second floor of the Bowman and Boardman's Store and later in the small village's wooden schoolhouse which was then located just west of Oakwood Cemetery. The first Methodist church building was begun in 1843 and was a red brick structure which stood for many years on the northside of East Second Street near Ottawa Avenue. By 1854, the congregation had outgrown the church building and plans were begun for a second church building which was finished in 1857. Constructed at a cost of $15,000, the West Second Street and South Peoria Avenue structure was dedicated on the first Sunday in January, 1858. In 1889, a third and larger building was constructed at a cost of $35,000.

EPISCOPAL CHURCH

Eighteen years after being organized in Dixon, the Episcopal Church of Dixon erected and dedicated their first house of worship in 1856. St. Luke's parish was organized by Rev. James De Puy (or De Pui) a missionary-at-large for the church in the Rock River Valley area. The religious group built a rectory on land donated to the church by "Father" John Dixon. Rev. De Puy was reportedly offered his choice of land in North Dixon if he would settle in the growing little community and start a church. The minister accepted the land offer and in 1837 built a small frame house now located at 608 N. Jefferson Avenue. The 1856 church building was replaced in 1871 with consecration ceremonies taking place on October 18, 1872. St. Luke's was valued at $16,800 when constructed including a 138-foot tall church spire that was destroyed in a lightning-started fire in 1907. The present church rectory which stands next door to the church was constructed, in part, with stone left after the construction of the Dixon Public Library in 1901.

LUTHERAN CHURCH

The history of St. Paul's Lutheran Church of Dixon began August 20, 1848 when services were held in a barn located on the John N. Burket farm east of Dixon for the 16 persons gathered to worship together. At first called the First Evangelical Lutheran Congregation of Lee County, the church later changed its name, in 1853, to St. Paul's Lutheran Church. At this time, the German portion of the congregation withdrew to form its own church, a separation that lasted until 1869. By 1855, the church group of 152 recognized a need for a formal church building. Consequently, a red-brick building was constructed at a cost of $4,000. Following the Civil War, increasing membership required a new building be built. In 1868, a brick structure 42 by 80-feet in size and two stories high was erected at the corner of West Second Street and Hennepin Avenue at a total cost, including fixtures, of $14,564. Shortly after this church was dedicated in 1869, the English and German segments of the membership were reunited. The second church building was used by local Lutherans until its new home was built and dedicated on April 25, 1954.

RIVERSIDE SHOE FACTORY

SHOE BUSINESS

The shoe industry and Dixon have survived together through good times and bad for over a century. This association of city and industry began early in 1887, when a group of local businessmen conducted a meeting with C.M. Henderson, a Chicago capitalist and Frank A. Watson, an experienced shoe production manager.

Watson, a former Dixonite, had convinced Henderson of Dixon's desire to see a large scale shoe manufacturing plant built in their community. After a series of meetings, it was decided that the local people should provide a plant site and $27,200 in cash with the Henderson Company providing an equal amount in shoe-making equipment.

At first protests were voiced from various quarters concerning the advisability of local monies being invested in such a project, B.F. Shaw, editor of the *Dixon Evening Telegraph,* noted the factory would hire 300 to 600 employees, put $200,000 into the community annually and even create a 25% rise in population.

By 1888, all areas of the shoe plant were in operation and in 1890, another part was constructed that came to be known as the Dixon Shoe Company. Not content with their recent endeavors, the local Businessman's Association signed the C.H. Fargo Shoe Company to an identical contract as given the Henderson Company four years earlier.

Two years earlier in 1892, shoe production at the Fargo plant began in a building build at 735 E. Second Street. It wasn't long before a skilled work force, receiving an average $10.00 per week wage, was employed at both Dixon shoe factories.

All was well in the shoe business in Dixon until 1896 when the directors of the Fargo Factory decided to dissolve and reorganize their firm. They managed to do so and were able to continue operations until shortly after the turn-of-the-century when C.M. Henderson Company bought their plant and shoe-making machinery.

FARGO SHOE FACTORY

This early photograph is interesting for several reasons. It shows the "First Chance - Last Chance Saloon" so named because it was a drinker's first opportunity to purchase a drink when traveling south and his last chance before crossing the Galena Avenue Bridge on the way north. The light pole to the right of the frame building carries a sign reading "Danger -Don't Hitch Here". The leather-wound pole was a favorite scratching place for horses as evidenced by the steed rubbing his nose. Too, the long leather fly strips can be seen over the back of the horse to the left.

PRIVATE CURRENCY

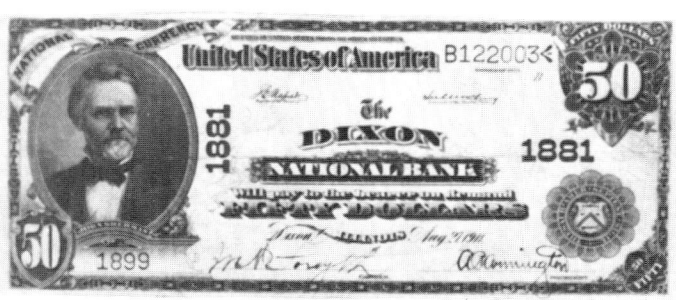

The Dixon Hotel Company issued its own private currency at Dixon's Ferry for several years. These bills had to be signed by both the President and Secretary of the organization, as well as having the bearer's name and the date filled in before being negotiable. Since they were not backed by the resources of a banking house or the Federal government, their worth was often suspect. The Dixon National Bank's national currency bills, too, required joint signatures of the financial institution's President and Cashier. As late as 1929 banks issued private currency. Also in 1929, the large size of paper was reduced to its present form.

FINANCIAL INSTITUTIONS

The story of Dixon's banking business is a long and interesting tale. As a formally established business, banking started in the community in the fall of 1846, when S. Noble and Company began operations. Silas Noble, Henry T. Noble and Jerome W. Hollenbeck owned a real estate firm that developed, in 1854, into this banking business at 108 West First Street. The same year, 1854, a private bank owned by Robertson, Eastman and Company of Rockford began at 202 West First Street with Samuel C. Eells joining the firm later in the year.

In 1855, when the Union Block (105-107 West First Street) was built, the banking firm of Noble and Hollenbeck with J.B. Nash as a partner moved into a ground floor office. This enterprise, named the Lee County National Bank, failed in the national panic of 1857.

E.B. Stiles started a bank in 1854 after being one of a group who constructed the Exchange Block at the southeast corner of East First Street and Galena Avenue. This enterprise, called the Exchange Bank, collapsed in the post Civil War 1864-65 period.

In 1865, the Lee County National Bank began again and was officially rechartered with original capital of $100,000. Joseph Crawford served as president with Samuel C. Eells, John Coleman and Joseph Utley holding executive positions.

On September 15, 1871, the Dixon National Bank started in an office on Galena Avenue and would go on to become Dixon's longest operating financial institution. The Lee County National Bank was rechartered, again, in 1885, and in 1911 opened its first new bank building.

In 1908, the Union State Bank was organized with J.B. Countryman as president. This bank built an imposing office structure at the northeast corner of West First Street and Peoria Avenue from which they operated until November, 1920, when they were closed due to a Federal bankruptcy action.

The Dixon Building and Loan Association started in June, 1887, with Attorney Sherwood Dixon as president. The lending association moved west on East First Street to the former location of the Giesenheimer Department Store (the "round corner block") at the northeast corner of East First Street and Galena Avenue in

The Dixon National Bank moved to its present building in 1914.

In 1896, the Dixon National Bank located in the Schuler Building at the corner of West First Street and Galena Avenue.

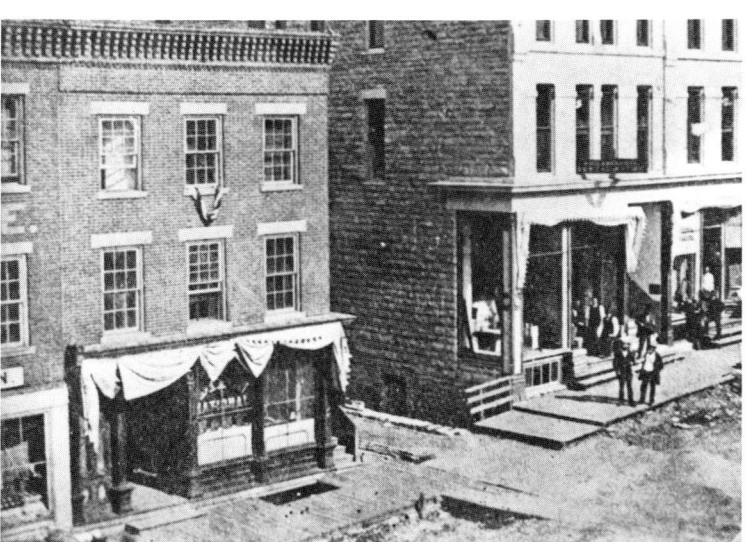

In the three-story building on Galena Avenue, the Dixon National Bank opened its first offices in 1871.

This 1920's photograph shows the location of the City National Bank.

the 1960's. Now known as Home Federal Savings and Loan, with its main office in Rockford, an additional local facility is maintained at 122 Boyd Street.

The Dixon National Bank moved to a new building location at the southwest corner of West First Street and Galena Avenue in 1896 and 18 years later in 1914, moved across West First Street to a spacious five-story "skyscraper" office building that continues today to be the home of the city's largest banking complex.

The Dixon Trust and Savings Bank operated in the community from 1929 to 1933 when it was liquidated by the Dixon National Bank and City National Bank through a joint agreement. The City National Bank built their current buiding in 1926 and saw Warren C. Durkes appointed its new president two years later.

The City National Bank was closed in March, 1933, as a result of the national banking holiday. In December of 1933, City National Bank in Dixon was organized and expanded along East First Street in 1965. In 1983, the bank was rechartered as a state bank and in 1986-87, as part of Premier Financial Services, Inc., Freeport, remodeled their facility.

The First Federal Savings and Loan Association, under Alden F. Hunter's direction, began in the community in 1956. A large modern financial facility, located on Dixon's north side at 413 North Galena Avenue, was built in 1974 for use by the Rockford owned savings and loan business.

The Dixon National Bank, with two branch banking facilities and under the long time leadership of Henry O. Lovett and Donald R. Lovett, holds the longevity record as being the community's oldest banking concern — 116 years of continuous independent banking service to Dixon and Lee County.

The Union State Bank, organized in 1908, made use of this imposing building until 1920.

The First Federal Savings and Loan Association was located at 105 West First Street for many years.

The northeast end of the Galena Avenue Bridge contained the Harry Cheverton and Son Market. Cheverton also acted as a toll tender collecting a dime for anyone who crossed the bridge.

This toll house was situated at the southwest end of the Galena Avenue Bridge. The toll tender, in this case Alex Turner, Sr., was allowed to operate his own business while collecting charges for use of the bridge. The boot and shoe repair business Turner operated augmented his salary as toll tender.

BRIDGES

The first Indians living in the valley of the Rock River crossed the rushing stream at what is now Dixon by any means available; swimming, wading, canoeing, ferrying or, in the winter months, by walking across the ice. Always an obstacle to progress and growth, crossing the Rock River was a constant challenge to early Indians and white settlers alike.

By the time (April, 1830) John Dixon arrived at the river, the "poling" method, whereby a boat was propelled across the stream by means of pushing it with long poles, was in use. Five years later, Dixon replaced this system with a rope ferry.

"Father" John Dixon was instrumental in the establishment of the first bridge built over the river in 1846. When put into use the bridge ended the part of his business enterprise that had earned him more than $800 the year before in crossing fees.

The 1846 bridge was constructed at a cost of $8,000 by the Rock River Bridge and Dam Company at the foot of Ottawa Avenue. It was the first of many toll structures that would cross the swirling waters.

This bridge lasted, with repairs to ice damage, until 1851 when a higher structure was completed. The wooden bridge and several like it lasted but a few months with each becoming victim of winter's ice and spring's floods.

The bridge built by Zachariah H. Luckey, at a cost of $12,000 in 1859, lasted four months. The 1861 Free Bridge, which had to undergo major repair after ice damage in 1866 and 1868, served for the decade of the 1860's.

At this time the people of Dixon felt a more lasting bridge should be constructed; one that flood water, ice jams, floating debris or washed-out dams could not take out or partially destroy on an almost annual basis. With this thought in mind, the Dixon City Council awarded an $80,000 contract to L.E. Truesdell to construct a 656-foot long iron double truss bridge over the Rock River.

The Truesdell Bridge was completed and opened to the public on January 21, 1869 with "Father" John Dixon leading a parade across the Galena Avenue structure. Surely all in the community echoed the thoughts of a newspaper writer who noted this bridge would stand "for a lifetime or more."

This hope was not to be, however, for during a baptismal ceremony just below the bridge on Sunday, May 4, 1873, the famed Truesdell Bridge collapsed, killing 46 persons.

In a moving story concerning one of Dixon's greatest disasters, the local *Dixon Sun* wrote:

> "It is no time, at such an hour as this, of desolation and woe, for us to discuss the question of responsibility for such a disaster. Hearts are too full of grief, eyes too full of tears to see the true weight of the horrible affair. Let us bury our dead peacefully, let us look up in trust to the future placing reliance upon the arm of Him who never forsakes His people in the time of trouble."

1862 - IRON RAILROAD BRIDGE

In the fall of 1873, the Howe Truss Wooden Bridge was built on the same piers as the Truesdell Bridge by the American Bridge Company at a total cost of $18,000. This structure stood for 12 years before being replaced in 1884 by a $35,000 bridge that would serve travelers over the Rock River for more than half a century.

The Galena Avenue Bridge was finally condemned and demolished in the summer of 1938 to make way for the present Abraham Lincoln Memorial Bridge span. Dedication ceremonies were held on October 5, 1939 for the Galena Avenue structure which was built by the State of Illinois at a total cost of $316,500.

In 1920, work was begun on a new railroad bridge over the Rock River to replace the structure that had carried trains and their traffic for 52 years since the refitting of the bridge with iron in 1862. Built of steel and resting on 15 concrete piers and two massive abutments, usage of the single track bridge was discontinued in 1987.

During the 1930 Dixon Centennial Celebration the newly constructed Peoria Avenue Bridge was dedicated as a memorial to the soldiers and sailors of Dixon and Lee County who had served their country in World War I. The bridge, built at an original cost of $166,000, was renamed the Ronald Reagan Bridge in 1978.

1873 - TRUESDELL BRIDGE DISASTER

1930 - PEORIA AVENUE BRIDGE (RENAMED RONALD REAGAN BRIDGE - 1978)

1939 - ABRAHAM LINCOLN MEMORIAL BRIDGE

ST. MARY'S SCHOOL

The first Catholic school in the community was located in a frame church building used for services from about 1854 to 1872. Classes were taught by the Dominican Sisters from Sinsinawa, Wisconsin. By 1897, the home of George L. Schuler had been purchased for $9,000 and remodeled for a grade school building. The first principal of the school was Sister Regina. The school was located on South Peoria Avenue between 7th and 8th Streets with over 200 children enrolled. A later two-story brick school building was constructed on the same site to be replaced by the current modern structure in the late 1960's.

DIXON TELEGRAPH

B.F. Shaw poses proudly (ninth figure from the right) with his delivery boys and staff in front of the building he purchased in 1880 to house the needs of the *Dixon Evening Telegraph*. The newspaper remained in this East River Street building for 14 years.

Elias Bovey is pictured standing next to the brick building facing Ottawa Avenue at Commercial Alley that served as the office for his extensive lumber yard business. Bovey's property extended from East First Street to East River Street and included the large brick edifice located at the corner of First and Ottawa Streets. That part of Bovey's property from Commercial Alley to River Street became the location, in 1939, of the Beier Bakery. The Bovey yards were a community landmark for decades. The wife of "Father" John Dixon's second son, John W. Dixon, lived in the small brick building after her husband died in 1847 until the middle 1850's when she moved with her father-in-law to a home in North Dixon.

JASON C. AYRES

Jason Cyrus Ayres, president of the Dixon National Bank for 43 years, was born in DePuyster, New York, on August 22, 1835. He "went west" at the age of 19 arriving at Chicago in 1854. Ayres traveled by railroad coach to Rochelle in 1855 and proceded the rest of the way to Dixon by stage coach. That same year young Ayres entered the real estate business by becoming an employee of Joseph Crawford and Company. He stayed with Crawford for 11 years leaving in 1866. He was both City Clerk and City Treasurer in Dixon for 20 years after becoming a lawyer in 1870. Ayres was one of the original stockholders and directors of the Dixon National Bank when it began in 1871, becoming president of the bank in 1881. In 1872, J.C. Ayres conducted the initial meeting of the Dixon YMCA in his office on Galena Avenue and would live to see the organization grow in size and importance in the community. He was active in all aspects of community life and held a multitude of civic and social posts and appointments. Jason C. Ayres died on January 1, 1924, at the age of 88 having been a resident of Dixon for over 70 years. Ayres lived through a period of time that extended from stage coaches to airplanes, from dirt streets to paved avenues, from primitive living conditions to up-to-date situations. He entered banking when that business was suspect by the average person and lived to see it grow to a trusted place in everyone's life.

AYERS OFFICE

FLOUR MILLS

Although flour mills had been a part of Dixon's industrial life since 1852, the Becker and Underwood Flouring Mills are the best remembered. Prior to 1852, most of the city's flour needs were met by transporting it from Galena at $2.50 per barrel or, later, purchasing it from Thaddeus Boardman's grist mill near Grand Detour.

In 1852, the first large flour mill in Dixon was owned and operated by J.B. Brooks and Colonel John Dement. Located at the south end of the existing Rock River dam, the five story stone mill cost $15,000 to construct.

1858 saw Charles Godfrey build another flour mill next to the Brooks-Dement structure. In 1870, Nathan Underwood and Henry Becker purchased the original and largest of the two mills. They introduced a method of producing flour they had learned of in Hungary. This method was named "Becker and Underwood New Process XXXX Flour."

1852 and 1858 flour mills constructed of limestone.

After fire of 1875 in which seven business places burned.

Nathan Underwood, Jr. proprietor of Becker and Underwood Mills.

In 1875, the huge mill was destroyed by fire. It was soon rebuilt only to be destroyed again by the ravages of fire five years later. This second fire, on April 4, 1880, killed two workers, injured at least ten and caused over $190,000 in damages.

In addition to the flour mill destruction, another mill, a flax bagging factory, a grist mill and part of a sash and blind factory suffered damages. The fire served notice on the community of Dixon that an adequate supply of water and trained firefighters were of prime necessity.

A Boston-based firm later purchased the flour mill for $53,000 and called it the Dixon Milling Company. An expansion program saw a seven-story facility constructed with steel and porcelain rollers in place of the huge old grindstones used over the years and electricity used in place of waterpower. The flour mill, turning out over 500 barrels of flour daily, continued for years to be a substantial part of Dixon's industrial picture.

Becker and Underwood Mills rebuilt after fire of 1875.

The scene after fire of 1880 which destroyed six factories, killed two men and injured ten and resulted in over $190,000 in damages.

Henry Becker, proprietor of Becker and Underwood Mills.

Becker and Underwood Mills with cooperage business circa 1881. The high water flood of 1881 can be seen with its resultant damage.

This unusual view of Dixon was taken by an unknown photographer in the mid-1870's. The early-day cameraman climbed the earthen embankment that carried the railroad tracks through town and posed his equipment somewhat north of the West First Street limestone arch overpass. The view he captured looks east toward the Dixon downtown area. A dirt covered West First Street can be seen on the right with Colonel John Dement's imposing home with its tall cupola on the left. In the distant skyline can be seen the Dixon Collegiate Institute on the left and three of Dixon's tall-steepled churches and the cupola of the Nachusa House.

JOHN DEMENT HOME

Colonel and Mrs. John Dement's home at the corner of West First Street and Madison Avenue in Dixon was built in 1855 by Alexander W. Pitts and owned by Elias B. Stilas, a local banker. The home was later purchased by Colonel Dement who lived in it until his death in 1883. At a later date, the large home with its four-story high cupola served as the office of the Lee County Power and Lighting Company before being demolished and replaced by the offices of the Illinois Northern Utilities Company. This photograph was taken of the Dement home during the high water flood of 1881.

WENDEL JEWELRY STORE

The George O. Wendel Store was located at 160 Galena Avenue for many years. In the photograph, Mr. Wendel is pictured in the center of the three men while Will Trein, who in later years would operate his own jewlery store in Dixon, is shown on the left. The Dixon YMCA, after 1872, rented reading rooms on the second floor as noted by the sign shown in the picture. The jewelry store, in 1896, became the home of the T.J. Miller Music Store.

Standing proudly in front of their general merchandise emporium, J. Bovey and Son pose for a local photographer. Located at 110 West First Street, the store's wooden walk, iron hitching post and ever-present platform scale can be noted as well as an array of the firm's other goods.

Bivins Star Grocery occupied the northeast corner of West First Street and Hennepin Avenue in the 1880's. The photograph shows the boardwalk in front of the frame store building, the double oil burning window lamps and a white bearded Mr. Bivins. The slogan of the business, in 1882, was "The Star Grocery Still Shines Supreme."

Dr. Webster W. Wynn owned this large single story brick home at the corner of West Third Street and Madison Avenue for many years. As a practicing physician in Dixon for decades, Dr. Wynn covered the greater Dixon area in the buggy pictured. His favorite horse is shown being held by Dr. Wynn's man servant.

DR. WEBSTER W. WYNN

THERON CUMINS

Theron Cumins, a partner of Major Leonard Andrus, operated the Grand Detour Plow Works which had been established in 1837 by John Deere and Andrus. After the death of Andrus in 1887, Colonel Henry T. Noble and Cumins took over the company moving it to Dixon in 1869. Cumins was active in the management of the plow making firm until his death in 1902. He left $15,000 to the Dixon Public Library upon his death.

JOSEPH UTLEY

Joseph Utley arrived in Dixon from New York in 1859 at the age of 44. He opened a saddlery and hardware store in town which he operated until 1867. When the Lee County National Bank opened in 1865, Utley was its first vice president and a member of its Board of Directors. He served as an Illinois State Canal Commissioner in 1869 and died in Dixon on March 19, 1889.

HENRY D. DEMENT

Henry D. Dement, the son of Colonel John Dement, was born in Dixon in 1840. He was educated locally and joined his father in various business enterprises before enlisting with the first group of Dixon volunteers on April 22, 1861, for service in the Civil War. By June of the same year, young Dement was promoted to First Lieutenant in Company A of the 13th Regiment of Illinois Volunteers. June, 1864, saw Company A return to Dixon following the end of the civil strife and Dement once again joined his father in business. In 1867, John Dement turned the ownership of the Dixon Plow Works over to his son and his partner, W.M. Todd. They operated the plow making factory for two years before selling it to F.K. Orvis and Company, Chicago. Dement's interest in education was great. He was a member of the Board of School Directors who built the first good school building in Dixon on the city's southwest side in 1868. In 1872, Dement was elected a Representative in the Illinois Legislature and in 1876, was chosen to represent Lee and Ogle Counties as an Illinois State Senator. For a time afterward, he served as Warden at the Joliet State Penitentiary and in 1880, was elected Illinois Secretary of State, a post he held until 1888. For many years, he and S.C. Eells operated the Dixon Flax Bagging Mill. Following the closing of the mill, Dement worked as post office inspector for Kane and adjacent counties for 14 years.

JAMES B. CHARTERS

The son of Governor Alexander Charters of Hazelwood, James B. Charters was born July 11, 1831, in Belfast, Ireland. He was educated in Ireland and studied for the law at Trinity College, Dublin. Charters came to Dixon in 1853 and in 1858 married Miss Fanny Charters, daughter of his uncle, Samuel M. Charters. Fanny Charters died in 1883. In 1877, Charters was elected Lee County Judge. He served one term as Mayor of Dixon and was one of the first directors of the Dixon Public Library. Charters died in 1902.

CHARTERS HOME

James B. Charters purchased this home from its first owner, Judge John V. Eustace. Constructed in 1852, the home was located at the corner of North Brinton Avenue and East Everett Street and covered an entire city block. Visitors of note at the large home included Abraham Lincoln, William Cullen Bryant, James Russell Lowell, and Margaret Fuller. The house, which faced East Everett Street overlooking the Rock River, was reduced in size over the years and finally torn down completely to be replaced by an equally stately edifice.

DIXON OPERA HOUSE

The fall of 1876 was a very special time in Dixon. The long anticipated opening of the Dixon Opera House was scheduled for late November. The last-minute arrival of a elegant drop curtain from St. Louis to complete the furnishings of the community's cultural and entertainment center made all involved with the project very nervous.

The Opera House, erected by H.J. Stevens, F.A. Truman, J.D. Crabtree and W.D. Stevens, would serve the city of Dixon for over 27 years. It was located on South Galena Avenue in the same location as the present Dixon Theatre building.

Opening night entertainment featured the talents of the Payson's English Opera Troupe. The complete success of the opening night entertainment in Dixon's Opera House was such that the previously used Union Hall on First Street was relegated to the sidelines.

The variety of entertainment presented down through the years was almost unlimited. Countless cultural notables entertained at the Opera House: Henry Ward Beecher, Susan B. Anthony, General Tom Thumb and his wife, the Hyer Sisters and the Barnabell Troupe. A never-ending variety of show business people whose lives were spent entertaining audiences "played Dixon."

The facility also served as host to reunions of the Illinois 13th Volunteer Regiment, conventions, parties and the like until the winter of 1920 when a fire completely destroyed the $40,000 building and ended forever the glory that once belonged to the Dixon Opera House.

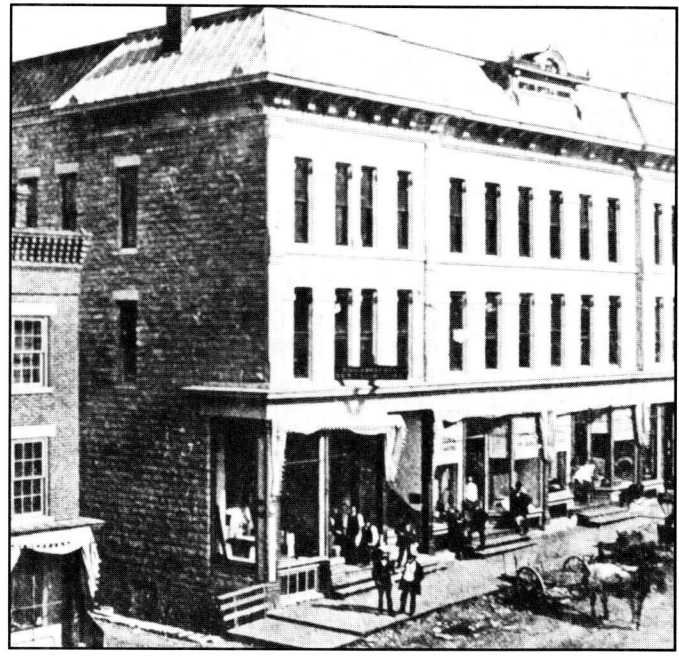

OPERA HOUSE - CIRCA 1880

OPERA HOUSE - CIRCA 1900

OPERA HOUSE STAGE

GRAND DETOUR PLOW WORKS

John Deere, a Vermont blacksmith, and Leonard Andrus of New York and Vermont, started the Grand Detour Plow Company in 1837. Locating in the tiny village six miles upstream from Dixon on the Rock River, both Andrus and Deere had moved west to secure new beginnings to their lives.

Andrus, in 1835, and Deere, in 1837, became residents of Grand Detour. Here they started in a small blacksmith shop with two forges to turn out whatever plows local farmers needed. Deere made a plow with a steel moldboard that could conquer the rich black dirt that covered the area.

Business was excellent but distribution of the finished plows was hampered by the lack of adequate transportation for distribution. In 1848, Deere withdrew from his partnership with Andrus and moved to Moline, Illinois, where he started a plow factory.

Andrus had several business partners in the plow business over the years and became very successful as well as wealthy in his business endeavors. A large factory was constructed in Grand Detour but burned to the ground in October, 1857. A new structure was erected and plows were once again turned out.

Major Andrus died in February, 1867. The plow business was then operated by Theron Cumins. Over the years Cumins became partners with Col. Henry T. Noble, Orris B. Dodge and Charles R. Noble.

The entire Grand Detour Plow Works was moved to Dixon in October, 1868, taking over the facilities that housed the Union Eagle Works since 1857. Located within a six-acre triangle-shaped area between the depots of the Chicago and Northwestern and Illinois Central Railroads, the factory soon employed over 200 workers.

A large fire in 1888 destroyed several buildings in the factory complex but recovery was speedy and the factory was once again producing plows at top capacity.

Thousands of plows and other farm implements were produced and soon the plow works had received world-wide fame

for the products they made.

By the turn-of-the-century, the Dixon factory consisted of more than seven buildings, employed 300 skilled workers and was a great contributor to the overall betterment of the Dixon area.

The Dixon Plow firm was sold in 1919 to the J.I. Case Company who operated it until closing the manufacturing business in the depression year of 1932.

LEE COUNTY JAIL

In 1872, after several experiences of prisoners escaping from the 1840 log jail building that stood on the northeast corner of East Third Street and Ottawa Avenue, the Lee County Board of Supervisors decided to build a new jail. At a county board meeting in February, 1872, Lorenzo Wood, a Dixon supervisor, offered a resolution that the board appropriate $18,000 with which to construct a new facility. A house and lot located at West Third Street and Hennepin Avenue, was purchased from Sarah Havens for $1,000 and the old jail and lot were sold for $2,500 with these monies being added to the construction fund. Foundations for the new jail were laid on April 25, 1872, as an addition to the existing house. The county approved an additional $516.88 for extra work and material including a wooden fence and a new outhouse near the jail building. The 1872 jail facility was considered one of the most modern and up-to-date structures of its kind when completed in November, 1872. The structure was in use for almost a century before being torn down and replaced with the modern Lee County Law Enforcement Building in the late 1960's.

For the first 41 years of its recorded history, Dixon was without a building to house any of the councils of government under which it operated. Rented facilities were always put into use during this period of time. The Lee County Courthouse and various public meeting places and rooms were utilized by the city fathers to conduct their official business.

Finally, in 1871, at a cost of $5,200, a new wood city hall structure was built on the corner of Hennepin Avenue and West Second Street. This photograph shows the new city hall and some of the proud volunteer firemen that made use of its facilities. The upper section of this first city hall had a large meeting room where training sessions and meetings for the volunteer firemen were held and where the first public library in Dixon was located.

The large bell tower to the left was rung to alert the local population of fire. Both the Dixon Hook and Ladder Company and the Monitor Hose Company made use of the new city hall building with equipment belonging to both shown in the picture.

OLD CITY HALL

DIXON WATER WORKS

An adequate water supply was always of prime consideration to citizens of Dixon since the very inception of the community. Water, not only for normal day in-day out home and business use but for protection against spreading fire, was considered the number one utility service needed for growth and protection.

By 1884, Dixon had grown in industrial, residential and commercial areas to the point where a fully functioning water works was desired. Eastern capitalists, who recognized the importance of water to the city, bonded the newly constructed $80,000 Dixon Water Works for $60,000 and sold all the bonds to east coast investors.

In the first few years the water works operated, it proved to be unprofitable and the out-of-state bond holders foreclosed and took possession of the River Street plant. A new company was then organized consisting of a number of Dixonites as stock holders. After the change of ownership, three artesian wells were dug furnishing the people of Dixon with water from depths of 1630, 1700 and 1810 feet.

The next few years saw over 12 miles of water mains laid with 98 fire hydrants located throughout the community. The Water Works stand pipe had a capacity of 270,000 gallons while the reservoir located next to the plant held over 500,000 gallons of water.

BREWERY BUSINESS

Clears Dixon Brewery was the enterprise of James D. Clears who constructed a large two-story brewery building of red brick between 1867 and 1869. A series of wooden additions were added to the original structure in the years following. In 1889, the plant's production capacity was over 500 barrels annually. Located at 166 East River Street below the site of the KSB Hospital, Clears Brewery served Dixon area beer and cider drinkers until the winter of 1912 when James Clears discontinued business.

The Dixon Brewery Company was started in 1871 by Conrad Thompson in a small brewery located at the corner of West 7th Street and Jackson Avenue in Dixon's western section. Later owners included Nicholas Plein, who owned a West First Street tavern for many years, and George Schorr.

The Dixon Brewery was also called the City Brewery over the years. One of the features of the Dixon/City product was their Lager Beer. In 1894, they advertised their product as being the "Best Lager Beer - Saloon And Private Families Supplied At Lowest Prices."

Another brewery, the Dixon Bottling Works, was a beer-making business located at 122 West First Street that operated for many years. In the 1890-1910 period the firm advertised: "C.H. Thomann and Brothers, Proprietors - Will Deliver To Any Part Of The City On Short Notice." The brewery produced "Milwaukee and Dixon Beers" that were a steady seller for their owners.

In 1905, George Schorr organized a $50,000 stock issue to obtain full control and modernize the Dixon Brewery Company. In 1908, Dixon voted to become a dry city, so Schorr started another stock company and changed the name of the firm to the LaSalle City Brewing Company. Schorr sold his brew out-of-town during Dixon's two dry years. As soon as the town voted wet again, he changed the name of his firm back to the Dixon Brewery and began selling his products in town.

On April 6, 1911, the brewery building at 7th Street and Jackson Avenue burned down but the 800 barrels (a two week supply) of beer stored in the basement survived the fire. A $90,000 property loss resulted for which Schorr carried only $12,000 in insurance. Schorr sued the city of Dixon and the Dixon Water Company for $35,000 claiming a lack of proper water pressure caused the fire to fully destroy his brewery. Nothing came of the court action and the brewery was later rebuilt. This was the last major fire to which horse-driven vehicles were dispatched. The animals were replaced that year with the city's first motor-driven fire fighting equipment.

The first retail grocery store in Dementtown was opened by William C. "Billy" Jones on December 23, 1886. Located on Depot Avenue, this photograph shows Jones Grocery in the mid-1890's after an expansion from the original 20 by 30-foot space next to it had taken place. Billy Jones, on the left, is shown with two of his customers and his delivery buggy and horse.

JONES GROCERY

FLAX BAGGING MILL

Dixon's pioneer entrepreneur, Colonel John Dement, established the first flax bagging operation in the United States. As with many of Dement's activities, once thought-out plans were rapidly advanced, buildings erected, equipment secured and manufacturing processes begun.

Dement's project was developed in 1865 just after the Civil War when cotton trading was beginning to recuperate from the effects of wartime. In the following year, a two-story native limestone mill was constructed on East River Street to make use of available waterpower for machinery use. By February, 1867, Dixon's Flax Bagging Mill, operated by Jerome and Downing, with Dement as the sole proprietor, was fully in operation.

The 75-foot long building was extended another 60-feet in 1870 in order to increase the capacity of the mill to over 3,000 yards of cotton bailing cloth per day. Fifty men, women and girls were employed processing in excess of 9,000 pounds of tow made from 36,000 pounds of flax straw that "took 25-30 acres to grow each working day of the week." Shipping two railroad carloads of flax bagging each week, Dement's mill sent products south to Memphis, Louisville and St. Louis where it was distributed throughout the southern cotton fields to wrap bails of cotton.

According to history sources, flax bagging continued until the late 1880's when the United States Congress removed tariffs on imported jute. Use of the cheaper imported material made it unprofitable to produce flax bagging for cotton bails.

DEATH OF "FATHER" DIXON

At the advanced age of 92, "Father" John Dixon died on July 6, 1876 in Dixon. He had lived in the community which bears his name for exactly half his lifetime. "Father" Dixon was 46 years of age when, in 1830, he and his family arrived at Ogee's Ferry.

The city's founder had been in failing health for a long time and his death was not unexpected. However, when word came of his passing, the muffled tones of church bells mournfully announced to the city's citizens its beloved founder was dead.

Ministers from all local churches took part in the funeral which was held the Sunday following Dixon's death. The Reverend Mr. Carnhman of the First Baptist Church, which "Father" Dixon had attended, gave the funeral eulogy.

Flags were hung at half mast throughtout the community for a week and stores and public buildings were draped in black. The Lee County Courthouse, where services were attended by from eight to ten thousand mourners, was draped in black.

The community of Dixon revered the old gentlemen who gave so much to the establishment and future growth of his namesake. "Father" John Dixon's name, forever intertwined with all aspects of city life, will always remind all who hear it of the white haired *Nadah-chu-rah-sak*.

The last known photograph of "Father" John Dixon was taken shortly before his death.

The Lee County Courthouse, on Sunday, July 9, 1876, was draped in black to mark the passing of "Father" John Dixon. Between eight and ten thousand mourners attended the public funeral services conducted by ministers from local churches.

Although "Father" John Dixon died July 6, 1876, and was buried within three days of his death in Oakwood Cemetery with all the honors a city, county and state could give a man of his stature and reputation, his grave went unmarked for 17 years. Through the efforts of the Ladies Oakwood Cemetery Association, a suitable lasting monument was placed over his grave. The 11 ton, 4½ by 5½ foot block of solid polished granite with a life-size bust of "Father" Dixon in bas-relief was purchased with funds raised by the local ladies. Dedication ceremonies took place in the summer of 1893.

"Father" John Dixon outlived his wife, Rebecca, and all of his children. After the death of her husband, John W. Dixon, son of the city's founder, Elizabeth A. Dixon made a home for her father-in-law. Elizabeth Dixon resided in this home, built in 1853, that was located at the southwest corner of North Jefferson Avenue and East Bradshaw Street. Originally sided with wide board planks, the home later was covered with grout; a mortar substance containing stones that could be later painted. Here "Father" John Dixon resided for the last 23 years of his life.

This interesting composite photograph of 13 leading Dixonites of an earlier era show Quartus Ely, merchant, in the center. The three men at the top of the picture, from left to right, are: Andrew Benjamin, merchant; Isaac Boardman, publisher; and David Welty, jurist. The three men on the left, from top to bottom, are: Ferris Finch, artist; Leander A. Devine, unknown; and Phillip M. Alexander, merchant. The trio of men on the right are: Henry Becker, industrialist; James L. Camp, postmaster; and Ozias Wheeler, sheriff. The three men on the bottom are: B.F. Shaw, editor; Martin H. Williams, veteran; and Andrew Benjamin, merchant.

These eight similing ladies joined together in the 1910-1915 era in Dixon for an afternoon of tea and conversation.

CHAPTER III

GROWTH YEARS

1890 - 1929

Dixon's 7,000 residents, just a decade before the arrival of the twentieth century, were part of an estimated 75,000,000 people nationally. The 1880's drew to a close with a general prosperity in evidence, as well as an increased desire to promote additional industrial expansion.

1890 saw the beginning of the Chautauqua movement in Dixon. Assembly Park came into being on the city's northeast side and, as each summer went by, its fame as a recreational and entertainment center grew.

The following year, Eichler's Bee Hive Store opened on Galena Avenue, Will Trein's Jewelry Store business started and George C. Loveland's F.X. Newcomer Company began. Retail activity was strong in the community as financial enterprises gained both strength in resources and civic involvement. When C.M. Henderson purchased the Lee County Power and Lighting Company in 1892, the public realized there was a need for local financial commitment.

Pleasure Park began in the year before Charles R. Walgreen, a young boy of 9, moved to town with his family and the *Dixon Evening Telegraph* moved into its new East First Street building. Firms such as the Anglo-Swiss Condensed Milk Company, Fargo Shoe Company, Henderson Shoe Factory and the A. Reed and Sons Piano Company were encouraged to locate in Dixon during this era.

The jewel in the crown of local industrial acquisition by the Improvement League, however, came in 1894 when the Reynolds Brothers Wire Screen Factory moved to Dixon from Cortland, New York. This firm was to be a major local employer for the next 68 years.

The Dixon National Bank, in 1896, after 25 years of friendly service to the area, moved across Galena Avenue to the George Schuler building. This was the year bicycles became popular both as a means of transportation and a social activity. The same year, Buffalo Bill and his Wild West Show appeared in Dixon, and the year Otto Beier opened his bakery and grocery store at the corner of West First Street and Hennepin Avenue.

Judge Solomon H. Bethea's gift of land, building and funds to equip the Katherine Shaw Bethea Public Hospital began a 90-year dynasty of high excellence in medical care for the community.

When Royal Jones opened his funeral home in Dixon in 1897, little did he realize that the Jones Funeral Home would continue to exist well into the 1980's. This was also the year Dixonites became aware of a growing tension in and around Cuba that would result in a full-fledged war within a year. The Spanish-American War of 1898 saw Company G of the Illinois National Guard leave Dixon to return again within the year after having fought in Cuba.

A year before the end of the 19th Century, George Squires, local entrepreneur, began the Dixon Paper Box Factory which the *Dixon Evening Telegraph* noted "was a busy and interesting place." Relocated two years later in the Brink and Deeter Planing Mill, the Squires company was capable of turning out between four and five thousand boxes daily. Also, in 1899, a young William H. Ware ("Billy") began a hardware store business at 211 West First Street that would last over 50 years.

As the century turned, dark stained oak furniture, leaded glass shaded lamps, heavy damask drapes and the latest in Hoosier Kitchen Cabinets graced the homes of Dixon. Times were good in Dixon. Industries were busy, employment was high and the 70-year-old city on the banks of the Rock River was eagerly anticipating the challenges of the twentieth century.

The dedication of the new Lee County Courthouse in 1901 gave notice to all that the first part of the new century was to be an interesting time in Dixon. A huge clear-span auditorium in Assembly Park was constructed and George H. Page purchased the historic Hazelwood Estate; two events that were of interest to all Dixonites.

The Dixon Public Library, an outgrowth of the book-lending system maintained by the local volunteer fire department, was built in 1901. O.B. Dodge and Theron Cumins, through generous bequests, made possible the building of the beautiful stone edifice.

Two major industrial employers began production in 1902. the Watson-Plummer Shoe Company and the Anglo-Swiss Condensed Milk Company were in full operation with each being responsible for countless thousands of dollars being expended in Dixon each year.

One of Dixon's more interesting buildings, the Odd Fellows Hall at Galena Avenue and East Second Street, was dedicated in April, 1903. The organization received $24,000 from the estate of C.F. Emerson to make the building a reality.

The American Wagon Company, makers of motor truck bodies as well as bodies for trailers and wagons, prospered in Dixon after the turn-of-the-century until well into the 1920's. Located in the far western section of the city, the limestone building used by the firm still stands. The factory's "8-in-1" convertible truck body was its top selling product. Their use of the slogan "Any Boy Can Make The Change From Any One Form To Any Other Form In One Minute" helped sell farmers, truckers and businessmen on the merits of their fine wooden vehicle bodies.

As the year went by, Dixon saw the likes of President Theodore Roosevelt as he passed through town, the revival antics of Reverend Billy Sunday and the on-going success of the firemen's running teams. Events such as the opening of the E.E. Dayton cigar factory, makers of the Snipe, Banti and Independencia 5¢ cigars, the Rodesch Piano Company and the Dixon Country Club all drew the attention of the local populace.

The cars of the Sterling, Dixon and Eastern Electric Railway were to be seen daily and the Dixon Home Telephone Company expanded its facilities throughout the area. The construction of the dam over the Rock River in the summer and fall of 1904 brought under control the rushing waters of the surging river. A power source for years to come, the building of the dam was a major event of that era. The advent of the Sandusky Portland Cement operation, E.K. Ortt's Clipper Lawn Mower Company and the Gossard Corset factory all portented well for Dixon.

The Dixon City Hall opened in 1906 to serve through the next 81 years while in the following year the Dixon YMCA opened to play an active role in the community for over 23 years. Three years later, the Federal Post Office was begun to be followed by the dedication of the $70,000 South Central Public School which replaced the old White Brick School that had stood for so many years until it burned.

Lowell Park, a gift to the city in memory of Charles Russell Lowell, became a vital and beautiful addition to the entire Dixon area. The Dixon Park District, long a group of consequence, has effectively managed the large land area under their jurisdiction for the benefit and pleasure of all local citizens.

The year 1911 marked the end of a long era in Dixon when the last of the large strong fire horses were retired from active duty by the Dixon Fire Department. An interesting phenomenon at this time was the proliferation of the self-propelled vehicle as the major means of transportation. The motor age had began.

Illinois Northern Utilities became the major power source for Dixon in 1912; the same year Harry and Walter Fulfs opened their popular confectionery. "Talkies" became the rage when both the Rose Theatre and the Dixon Opera House began to feature movies on a regular basis. The Loveland School, opened in 1913 at a cost of $6,000, would educate Dixon children for many years.

When the Dixon National Bank moved across West First Street to their brand new five-story skyscraper bank building, Dixon knew their place in the sun was secure. Not only did the $100,000 edifice reflect the strength of the financial institution but demonstrated its faith in the future of the community.

F.W. Woolworth's first store opened in downtown Dixon in 1914 and the Dixon Chamber of Commerce, an outgrowth of the local businessmen's league, began a long history of service to the area. Dixon's own circus, Coop and Lent's, spent the winter of 1916-17 in Bovey's Sheds on East River Street, Oscar Coss started a dairy to distribute milk throughout the community and the news of the arrival in Dixon of The Illinois Colony for Curable Epileptics all made a great impact on Dixon at the time.

The advent of World War I brought change, if not physical at least in attitude, as Dixonites realized their country's power and prestige in world politics. When President Woodrow Wilson asked Congress for a declaration of war in April, 1917, more than 4,744,000 Americans were destined to take part in "the war to end all wars." Of this total over 1,500 men and women from Lee County answered their country's call to duty with Dixon contributing 382 of the total. Some 50 of those brave young men died in action or from wounds and diseases on the various battlefields of Europe.

An armistice with Germany was signed November 11, 1918, a day of great joy and celebration in Dixon. Those who returned following the terrible conflict marched proudly in May, 1919 under a wooden arch built to span Galena Avenue between the Lee County Courthouse and the Post Office near the Nachusa House. Inscribed on the Victory Arch were the words:

> *"A Grateful People Pause In Their Welcome To The Victorious Living To Pay Silent Tribute To The Illustrious Dead."*

Returning veterans saw the opening of "The Colony" on North Brinton Avenue, the arrival in Dixon of Henry M. Hey to begin a family ice cream making operation in Dixon that still exists and the October 28, 1919 adoption of national prohibition (The Volstead Act) as "The Great Experiment."

An event that would cause great joy and pride in Dixon 60 years later occurred early in 1920. At this time, Jack and Nell Reagan and their sons Neil ("Moon") and Ronald ("Dutch") moved from Tampico where young Dutch had been born on February 6, 1911. During the decade of the 20's, Dutch Reagan attended South Central Grade School, graduated from Dixon's North Side High School in 1928 and spent the summers from 1926 through 1932 as a Lowell Park lifeguard where he saved the lives of 77 swimmers trying to fight the Rock River's swift currents.

In this same era, the office of District #2 of the Illinois Division of Highways was moved from Moline to Dixon. The first staff of the new Dixon office, located in the Dixon National Bank building, consisted of Engineers H.F. Surman, O.F. Goeke, C.W. Ross and O.L. Gearhart.

Dixon, in the early 1920's, welcomed the Brown Shoe Company to its industrial picture, the A & P Grocery to its retail community and the business enterprises of Frank Kriem and Walter C. Knack to their midst. The Dixon Opera House fire destroyed a well known community landmark and made way for the construction of the Dixon Theatre.

Changes in downtown Dixon continued either through calamity or through planned growth. The John W. Duffy Garage, located in the George J. Downing Building on East First Street, where Kline's Department Store is now, suffered a $108,770 fire, on Christmas Eve, 1924, that destroyed over 60 automobiles then in storage. The next year saw the demise of the electric railway system in Dixon due to the increasing popularity of the automobile and Dement Schuler's Home Lumber Company announced a new home construction department to further enhance home ownership in the community.

A city meeting early in the 1920's produced this following list of "needs" many felt necessary to make Dixon a better community in which to live, work and play: "Pure milk supply; Rest rooms for visitors; Consider need for another bridge; Foster infant industries; Community cooperation; Encourage better amusements."

The mid-1920's saw a beautiful Knights of Columbus Home put into use, the City National Bank in Dixon celebrate the re-construction of their banking facility at a Washington's Birthday open house in 1926 and the construction of both the Elks Club and the large Dixon Country Club building. On December 30, 1927, local Masonic Lodge members dedicated their new northside Lodge that had been a gift of Colonel William Brinton.

St. Anne's Church, a $55,000 structure located on East Morgan Street, began service to the 80 Catholic families on Dixon's north side on July 28, 1929. Dixon High School was dedicated on December 13, 1929. The school became known as one of the most beautiful high school campus facilities in the mid-west.

As the automobile grew in popularity, a cry for more and better roads was heard across the land. "Get Illinois Out Of The Mud" was a slogan used locally to increase public awareness for the need for better farm-to-market roadways. Illinois law makers, the Illinois Department of Transportation and local officials were proud, in 1924, to see Illinois Route 2 between Rockford and Sterling through Dixon receive a great deal of attention.

In 1929, the year Beier's Bakery celebrated their 60th anniversary in business and Charles R. Walgreen purchased the beautiful Hazelwood Estate, an event of lasting impact on the future of Dixon and the entire nation took place. This was the Wall Street stock market crash on October 29, 1929 when 16,410,000 shares of stock were sold at a loss estimated at $8,000,000,000. Thousands of investors would see their fortunes wiped out over night. The resultant shock waves reverberating throughout the Dixon community as the decade of the 1920's came to an end.

COMPANY G

Dixon's Company G, 6th Regiment, Illinois National Guard, was an active military organization for many years. In 1894, the group of volunteer soldiers saw service during the Pullman strike in Chicago organized by the foremost union organizer of his time, Eugene V. Debs. President Cleveland called out the National Guard along with Federal troops to control the strike by the powerful American Railway Union.

In April, 1898, Spain declared war on the United States. Patriotic enthusiasm swept the nation and made an impact on the men of Dixon. So much so, that on April 26, 1898, over 100 men of Company G left the community for service in Cuba and Puerto Rico. They returned after what was called "a splendid little war" in November, 1898.

Company G, on August 13, 1895, halted their training program at Camp Lincoln long enough to have a group photo taken.

The telephone arrived in Dixon in 1881 when the Western Union Telegraph Company installed the first phone in the city. Within a month 44 telephones were in use in Dixon. L.D. Pitcher headed a group of local investors who bought out the Western Union services and formed the Lee County Telephone Company. By 1902 over 700 telephones were installed in Dixon. Two years later, the Lee County Company became the Dixon Home Telephone Company. In 1904, competition arrived in the form of Central Union Telegraph Company with the majority of business places and factories using two telephones to receive and place calls. The Central Union, in 1912, with only 12 subscribers, went out of business. Located on the second floor of the I.B. Countryman Building on Galena Avenue for many years, a 1916 fire forced the Home Telephone Company to move its quarters to the second floor of the Schuler Building at the corner of Galena Avenue and West First Street. The telephone company built a new facility at the corner of West Second Street and South Peoria Avenue in 1917 and has continuously resided at that location.

DIXON HOME TELEPHONE COMPANY

MOSS BUILDING

The Moss Building at 214 West First Street has been put to a full range of use since its construction. As noted in the photograph it was once the location of the J.D. Appleford and Son buggy, hardware and plumbing supply business and the offices of *The Sun*, a longtime Dixon newspaper. The building at one time housed a double-alley bowling lane, owned by A.U. Thomas, in its basement while the Star and Rose Theatres were both located on the first floor over the years. Currently housing professional offices, a bakery and shoe repair business, the structure continues to serve Dixon citizens.

B.F. SHAW PUBLISHING

The *Dixon Evening Telegraph*, having outgrown its riverfront headquarters in which the paper had been printed since 1880, moved to this spacious two-story rock and stone building in 1894. Located at the southwest corner of East First Street and Ottawa Avenue, the building's front was of "unhewn red sandstone of unique design." The building was 25 by 60 feet in size and would serve the needs of the community well into the middle of the next century.

E.L. Kling was a pioneer Dixon jeweler who arrived in Dixon in the 1870's. He was also an ardent athlete and is shown here with his high-wheeler bicycle in a formally posed photograph.

The Dixon Power and Lighting Company was established after its management had purchased the electrical business developed by Charles M. Henderson. Henderson had initially furnished electrical power to his shoe factory enterprise and then to business locations and homes in the immediate area. His purchase of the power company, in 1892, gave the concern the honor of being the first company to operate under a franchise given by the City of Dixon. The new company purchased the Becker and Underwood Flour Mill building for use as a powerhouse in 1893 and installed a hydro-electric generator as a source of power. The Dixon Power and Lighting Company merged with the Illinois Northern Utilities Company in 1912 and later became part of the Commonwealth Edison Company.

CAHILL AND COWLES

The Dixon Power and Lighting Company, founded in 1892, had the services of William Cahill and Perry Cowles to assist the firm in keeping their customers supplied with adequate electricity. High above Commercial Alley, a local photographer captured forever on film the pole climbing teams of Cahill and Cowles "doing their thing."

E.J. RYAN'S GROCERY

This easily recognized downtown Dixon landmark was the home of E.J. Ryan's Grocery and Bakery when this photograph was taken. Ryan, his wife and a mustached customer are posed at the entrance of their store located at 206 West First Street. Together with their horse-driven delivery buggy, the Ryans were often seen in and around Dixon delivering their wares to residential customers. Although certain architectural embellishments have been removed from the facade of the building, the fanciful carving between the two upper windows on the red brick structure can still be seen.

H.O. Wheeler's business was located on the north side of the 100 block of West First Street for many years. He conducted a laundry, dyeing and cleaning business along with a gentleman's hair cutting enterprise as a sideline. Wheeler posed, with his barber assistant and his trained dog which stood up for the photographer, in front of his store sometime in the early 1890's. In the rooms above Wheelers, Mrs. Reynolds had dressmaking parlors and F.F. Dixon, "Knight of the Shears", conducted a merchant tailoring business.

H.O. WHEELER

I.B. COUNTRYMAN

The I.B. Countryman Meat Market was located on the west side of South Galena Avenue in the location that would later accommodate the Manhatten Cafe. A load of block ice can be seen on the boardwalk in front of the store. The ice was to be used in the storage of the market's meat supply.

CONDON AND JONES GROCERY

Condon and Jones Grocery was located at 17 First Street for several years. This late summer photograph shows the store's supply of fresh watermelons. The hitching post, boardwalk and dirt streets were familiar sights in downtown Dixon in the 1890's.

DIXON COAL YARDS

A fixture for many years in Dixon, the Dixon Coal Yards were located at the southeast end of the Galena Avenue Bridge. Mr. Edwards, the firm's owner, is shown here posing for the photographer on the bright sunny day. The coal yards also handled fuel oil and repaired furnaces for their customers. Today, the Dixon Chamber of Commerce occupies the same location.

EICHLER'S STORE

The Bee Hive, 158 South Galena Avenue, opened February 14, 1891, in what was then called the Jordan Building. Max and Adolph Eichler are pictured in the doorway of their store. The identity of the other five Dixonites is not known. The Eichler brothers moved their store to 119 West First Street in 1900 and in 1914 opened an annex across the street. By 1930, Eichler's covered all three floors of their 119 West First Street location. A large new retail outlet at 215-217 West First Street was opened on March 17, 1946, under the guidance of Victor and Joseph Eichler, sons of the founders. This store remained a vibrant part of downtown Dixon until the early 1970's.

JULIAN BARBER SHOP

This interesting building housed the John Julian Barber Shop at 107 South Galena Avenue. Julian, on the left, is shown with John Bales and Henry Trevane in front of his shop in the late 1800's.

MALLOY ROOMS

An enterprising Edward Malloy operated both the Exchange Pool Room and Exchange Sampler Room in this building at 10 West First Street in the 1890 - 1900 period. Larry Timmons, in black tie, vest and long white apron, was the bartender posing for the photographer. In second floor rooms, Dr. W.W. Wynn and Dr. Henry E. Paine conducted a medical practice while M. Cahill, merchant tailor, shared space at 9 West First Street.

O.H. BROWN DRY GOODS

O.H. Brown arrived in Dixon in 1890 to open a retail store in the Opera House Block on Galena Avenue. After three years in town, he purchased the three-story brick building constructed in 1888 at 101 West First Street from the Van Epps family and moved his extensive inventory to it. Brown later sold the building to Judge Crabtree and it was from the Crabtree Estate that the Dixon National Bank, in December, 1912, purchased the building. Brown and other occupants were given notices to vacate the building as it was to be torn down to become the location of the new five-story Dixon National Bank building. The bank had paid $30,000 for the 50 by 70-foot lot and would spend another $70,000 to build their new banking quarters. Brown moved his business back to Galena Avenue and re-opened the O.H. Brown Dry Goods Store at 121 South Galena Avenue on March 15, 1913.

SALZMAN MEAT MARKET

John Salzman owned and operated a meat market at 135 South Galena Avenue for several years. His store was second from the corner of Galena Avenue and West Second Street next to Dr. Stephens, a dentist, and Rowland's Drug Store. Salzman, shown in his butcher's apron, was a long-time Dixon merchant.

John Salzman, pictured here in June, 1915, was a butcher like his father before him. He cut fresh meat in the Weigle Meat Market on Hennepin Avenue for many years and also was employed as a butcher at the Reynoldswood complex west of Dixon.

Whatever secrets were being shared by the two horses pictured nose-to-nose in front of H.E. Donaldson's Drug Store at 12 West First Street in the early 1890's will never be known. The five dapper gentlemen standing on the wooden sidewalks of the store located to the left of the O.H. Brown Store pose elegantly for the photographer. Note the ornate mortar and pestle atop the tall hitching post in front of the drugstore.

SOLOMON H. BETHEA

KATHERINE SHAW BETHEA

KATHERINE SHAW BETHEA HOSPITAL

In the summer of 1895, Judge Solomon Hicks Bethea purchased and donated to the city the site of Katherine Shaw Bethea Hospital in memory of his wife. The first building constructed as a hospital in Dixon provided 17 beds and facilities for medical, surgical and obstetrical cases. Erected in 1896, the hospital began serving the community on January 5, 1897. In 1913, a third story was added as was a south wing. This addition increased the bad capacity to 40 and was made possible by the bequest of Miss Elizabeth Shaw, sister of the original donor. In 1926, another building was completed to the north adding 15 rooms, two solariums and an X-ray laboratory. A $130,000 west wing was completed in 1941.

In 1896, the 28 members of the Dixon Drum Corps posed proudly for this photograph. No local or area parade was complete without the addition of this popular all male marching group. As 16 drums are shown in the picture, it can be assumed there were than many drummers in the squad. Eleven of the members either played the fife or bugle, carried a flag or banner or led the organization as drum major. The young gentleman in the second row holding the broom and dust pan probably led the marching outfit at a good distance whenever they had the misfortune to follow behind a mounted horse group in any parade.

The Dixon College football team of 1900 was a powerhouse. The eleven man squad, complete with a backfield wearing face masks, played at the Dixon College Athletic Park. This large field covered an area over 300 yards by 400 yards, was fully fenced and could seat seven to eight hundred spectators in its grandstand. A scoring record was set by the local college football team (wearing the black and yellow colors of the school) when they soundly beat the DeKalb College football crew 152 to 0. Dixon's score included 27 touchdowns (rated then at 5 points each) and 17 field goals (each scored as one point). Note the round ball used by the team pictured in action above.

By 1895, the Rock River dam was showing the wear and tear caused by millions upon millions of gallons of water flowing over it for almost half a century. It was obvious at this time that a new dam was greatly needed.

Building the 1904 dam over the Rock River took the combined labor of 187 men and the assistance of 30 teams of horses. They worked just over six months to finish the mighty structure.

A steady stream of rushing water passes over the original 1848 dam in this 1880's picture. High above the bluff on the far side of the river can be seen the Dixon Collegiate Institute.

ROCK RIVER DAM

The need for the dam across the Rock River at Dixon was recognized shortly after "Father" John Dixon arrived to found the community in 1830. It was not until 1844, however, that there was enough interest in constructing a dam. The Dixon Dam and Bridge Company was formed for the purpose of building a dam, but it was not until 1848 that the Rock River Hydraulic Company accomplished the task at a cost of $1,500. Built of bricks, young trees, stone and gravel, the dam required constant attention and repair. The first use of waterpower serviced a sawmill located on the north end of the structure. As the south side of the river along East River Street saw more factories being built, additional water driven power was made available.

The Dixon Power and Lighting Company, in 1899, strengthened the existing dam to make it more compatible with the new hydro-electric plant then in use. From June to November, 1904, a new 720-foot dam, 24 feet wide at the base, was constructed. When completed, the dam increased electrical capacity to 2,000 horsepower. The Lee County Power and Lighting Company razed the hydro-plant in 1924 to make way for a new facility.

In 1907, the Illinois Northern Utilities Company constructed the first steam generating plant on the Rock River producing 3,000 kilowatt hours of electricity a day.

Dixon's electrical needs were furnished by the Illinois Northern Utilities until 1950 when the company merged with Public Service Company of Northern Illinois and became known as the Illinois Northern Division.

The bulkhead near the powerhouse of the Lee County Power and Lighting Company is shown when the Rock River dam was under construction. It became a popular place in the summer and fall of 1904 to walk and watch construction progress.

The old dam, built in 1848, was left in place when the 1904 structure was built. The new dam was constructed just below the old for added strength.

Following completion of the dam in 1904, factories such as Reynolds Wire Company, Dixon Power and Lighting Company, C.D. Parsons, Stewart Press and others along East River Street made use of the electricity and waterpower provided.

CHARLES H. HUGHES

A native of Berwick, Pennsylvania, Charles H. Hughes was born April 18, 1844, and arrived in Illinois in 1868 to become a farmer in Palmyra Township. Here he met and married Hannah Wilson. His long years of public service began in 1876 when he was elected Assessor of Palmyra Township. In 1879, he was elected Palmyra Township Supervisor, followed in 1886 by his election as Lee County Treasurer. Hughes moved to Dixon in 1892, was elected Mayor of Dixon three years later and was chosen as an Illinois State Representative in 1900. Charles Hughes was elected Illinois State Senator in 1902 and through his efforts both the Medusa Sandusky Cement Company and the Reynolds Wire Company located in Dixon early in the century. Senator Hughes also served as a Director of the Dixon National Bank, President of the Dixon Loan and Building Association and Commissioner of Lowell Park. When Senator Hughes died on May 12, 1907, he was Cashier of the Dixon National Bank.

A vast amount of land was utilized by the cement plant to produce the 1,500 barrel-per-day production of Medusa brand cement. At first 200 men were employed working with 6 kilns to earn an annual total payroll of over $200,000. Huge steam driven equipment was used to remove rock from the vast quarries and an extensive track and road system was constructed within the quarries to move equipment about the area.

In 1905, the Sandusky Portland Cement Works, through the efforts of Senator Charles H. Hughes and Attorney E.H. Brewster, decided to build a $750,000 cement producing plant along the Rock River near Dixon. Ground was broken in March, 1906, with production beginning in 1907.

In 1908, this group of hard-working men paused in their labors for the photographer. They were building a large addition to the Reynolds Wire River Street Plant that summer.

For over 68 years, the Reynolds Wire Company was an important part of the industrial life of Dixon. The makers of wire screen cloth ("Western Made For Western Trade") was established in Dixon in 1894 after a visit by Horace G. Reynolds in April of that year. Senator Charles H. Hughes, a loyal booster of Dixon, was instrumental in introducing the industrialist to the benefits of a Dixon location as well as arranging for community financial assistance to the wire cloth firm. The Reynolds factory was located in the large East River Street structure formerly owned by the Dixon Plow Works. The company made good use of the waterpower available from the Rock River. At first, the firm made window screen wire cloth, the first venture of its kind west of New York. Growth was rapid, expansion of the plant and its facilities were made almost on an annual basis and employment was large and steady. Later items produced included corn poppers and fly traps as well as a long listing of wire cloth products. A second building on East Second Street was later acquired to further expand production capabilities. In 1950, the company became a part of National Standard Company of Niles, Michigan, who operated in Dixon for 12 years before closing the Reynolds Wire Company operation.

The Reynolds Wire Company River Street Plant is seen in this fanciful artist's rendering. Used for advertising and publicity, the drawing was pictured on a post card highlighting the merits of Reynolds' wire cloth products.

REYNOLDS WIRE

LOWELL PARK

Charles Russell Lowell, Jr., in 1859, acquired 201 acres of heavily forested land along the banks of the Rock River upstream from Dixon. His reasons for making the purchase have never been definitely known but it was most probably partly for investment and partly because of the natural beauty of the area itself.

Lowell, an employee of the Illinois Central Railroad, was given the duty of securing the land for the further development of the rail system throughout Illinois and Iowa. Shortly before he bought the land that would later become Lowell Park, some timber had been cut for fuel used in the construction of the Illinois Central Railroad and part of the bottom land near the river had been cleared and put into cultivation.

Born in Boston, January 2, 1835, Lowell was married to Josephine Shaw Lowell in 1863. He was a Colonel of the Second Massachusetts Cavalry and a Brigadier General of United States Volunteers in the Civil War. About a year after his marriage, he was killed at the Battle of Cedar Creek, Virginia. For the rest of her life until her death in New York City in 1905, Josephine Shaw Lowell was interested in charities. Little charitable work in New York was conducted without her assistance.

Following her death at the age of 62, her daughter, Carlotta Russell Lowell, carried out her mother's wish by presenting the land above Dixon to the city for a public park.

As there was no law in Illinois at the time by which a city could own park land which was not within or adjacent to the city, Senator Charles H. Hughes introduced a bill in the Illinois legislature which was later passed, removing this restriction.

With the exception of Dixon Mayor I. Frank Edwards and one or two others, the city council of Dixon opposed accepting this land as a gift.

One member of the council was quoted in the *Evening Telegraph* as saying, "It is nothing but a big pile of brush and would only be a care and worry to the city."

Other objections included the fact that "every place along the river is a park anyway and no more are needed." Also noted was the fact that "this land is so far away from town that only the rich who have horses and carriages could enjoy it."

The objections, however, were overcome in short order for on April 4, 1907, the city council passed an ordinance establishing the gift of land as a public park to be known as "Lowell Park," owned and maintained by the City of Dixon.

The first Lowell Park Commission had as members A.C. Bardwell, E.N. Howell, Edward Vaile, Charles G. Smith and Charles H. Hughes. The Commissioners served without pay and were the forerunners of the elected membership of the Dixon Park Board.

Citizen participation played an important part in the early establishment of Lowell Park. In August, 1907, the first of many annual "Clean-Up-Days" were held. Over 100 local citizens spent the day in the park cleaning out an immense amount of deadwood, brush, stumps and trash. In later years, sometimes 6,000 or more people would show up to enjoy activities in the park after spending time cleaning and working in it.

For the past 128 years that the recorded history of Lowell Park has been available, the park has grown in size and importance to the people who enjoy its beauty and used its facilities.

Whatever its future, Lowell Park stands as a constant memorial not only to Lowell and his wife but to the hundreds of thousands who have, in so many ways, helped to guard and protect its natural beauty.

May 2, 1902, marked the first beginnings of BPOS Lodge No. 779 in Dixon. The initial clubroom of the Elks Club was on the third floor of the West First Street and Galena Avenue building then housing the O.H. Brown Dry Goods Store. The second site was located in the Bovey Building at East First Street and Ottawa Avenue. On June 13, 1911, the Elks Lodge voted to buy property located at South Ottawa Avenue and East Second Street then owned by W.N. Johnson of Chicago, and known as the Dr. Everett property. The present clubhouse cornerstone was laid on March 11, 1912, with dedication of the building taking place in 1913 when the Elks Lodge received its corporate papers. Membership in the Lodge went from 273 in 1911 to 408 in 1912 when the Elks Club opened for membership participation. This early photograph of the Dixon Elks Club dates back to the winter of 1913.

ELKS CLUB

PLEASURE PARK

"Pleasure Park Is No More."

"The Field which has been the scene of many pretty races, the Speedway where numerous fast horses have had their early time, the Park where many athletic struggles, baseball and football contests, have been won and lost during the past 12 years is to be cut up into city lots and to future generations will be known only as a neat residence district overlooking the river and the city beyond."

So read the January, 1905 *Dixon Evening Telegraph* obituary of what had once been the center of outdoor entertainment for Dixonites, their friends and their visitors for over a dozen eventful years.

It was E.C. Parsons, who in 1893, had laid out a half-mile dirt race track on land he then owned along the north bank of the Rock River. Pleasure Park, surrounded by acre after acre of unencumbered land, was a landmark of which the city was then justly proud.

The first society horse racing meet was held on July 4, 1894, when a colt named "Delmont" won a fast paced mile in 2:18½.

Other events held at Pleasure Park over the years included the Illinois State Fireman's Association's meetings and tournaments, bicycle and foot races, high school field events, baseball and football games and marching drill competitions. The Dixon Gun Club conducted clay pigeon shoots. Barnum and Bailey's, Sell Brothers and Forepaugh's circus attractions also appeared at Pleasure Park as did the famed Buffalo Bill Wild West Show.

The East Chamberlin Street entrance to the Rock River Assembly Park was a busy place through many summers. The official assembly bus or horsedrawn wagon holding a dozen people made frequent round trips between the grounds and downtown Dixon.

ROCK RIVER ASSEMBLY

The first chautauqua program was held in the summer of 1874 at Chautauqua Lake, New York, featuring an address by President Ulysses S. Grant. Fourteen years later, at the suggestion of Reverend John M. Ruthrauff of Dixon's Lutheran Church, the initial local program was held at Governor Charter's Hazelwood estate.

The Rock River Assembly came into being after Lloyd's Park on Dixon's northeast side along the banks of the Rock River was purchased at a cost of $5,531.21 for 34.15 acres by area churches. The 1890 meeting of the Rock River Assembly was held in a large temporary tent. The following summer a 110 by 75-foot wooden tabernacle, a three-story hotel, bath houses and other facilities

The three-story Bluebird Hotel was built in 1891 on the grounds of the Rock River Assembly overlooking the river. A busy place each summer season, the frame hotel was constantly filled with visitors.

The Old Settler's Memorial Log Cabin contained logs, fixtures and many pieces of memorabilia from Lee County pioneers. Dedicated August 15, 1894, the log cabin was a landmark in Assembly Park until the Lee County Historical Society moved it to its present location near the famous "Lincoln - The Soldier" statue in 1969.

were erected. The large tabernacle building served until 1899 when a circular auditorium was built at a cost of $7,000.

In 1895, the Rock River Assembly grounds were improved with the planting of 100 large trees and over 2,500 smaller ones. An on-going effort was made to attract the finest entertainment of the day to perform at the Assembly Park auditorium.

The rising cost of entertainers and lectures together with costs of advertisement and maintenance soon translated into ever-increasing debt. It soon became necessary to mortgage the entire Rock River Assembly property. By 1920, the debt had increased to over $30,000 and a decision to foreclose on the property was made.

Many of the summer homes constructed on the grounds of the Rock River Assembly have been moved to alternate locations in and around Dixon and are today private residences.

A rare interior view of the auditorium shows part of a typical audience. The building cost $7,000 to construct.

This huge auditorium, a clear-span circular facility that held thousands of spectators, was designed by Dixon architect Morrison H. Vail. Later used as a roller skating rink ("The Dome"), the wooden structure was completely destroyed by fire on Thanksgiving Eve, 1940.

J.D. VAN BIBBER

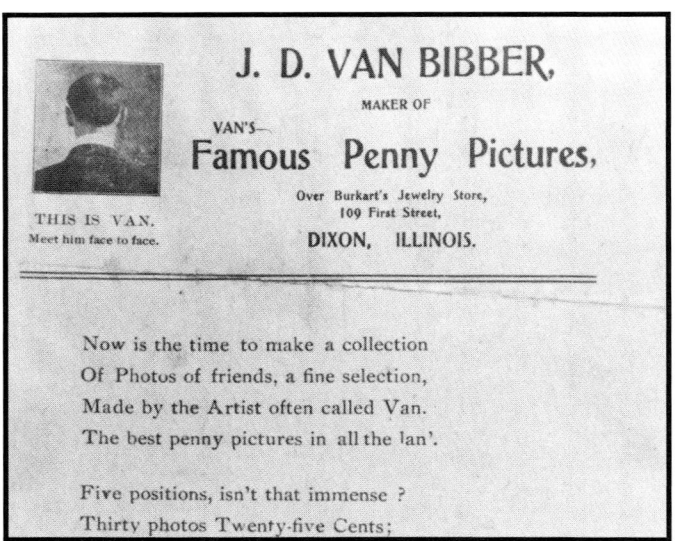

Van Bibber's "Famous Penny Pictures" were advertised by means of cards such as this. The unusual reverse picture of the gallery's owner and his poetic advertising are both of note on this early advertising card.

John D. Van Bibber came to Dixon from Davenport, Iowa, in 1901, to establish a photography gallery at 109 West First Street. He had been born July 17, 1873, in Scott County, Iowa. Van Bibber's photo gallery featured 30 small pictures for 25¢; an advertising gimmick that insured both financial success as well as notoriety.

He married Clara Jurgens, Rock Falls, on January 1, 1902. Van Bibber was elected a member of the Dixon City Council in 1911 and six years later was appointed Dixon Chief of Police, a position he held for 28 years until his death in 1945. At the time of his death, he was the oldest active chief of police in the state of Illinois both in point of age and in length of service. In 1984, an endowment to provide scholarships in his honor for the Department of Criminal Justice, Art and Allied Health at Sauk Valley College was provided by his son, John V. Van Bibber of Iowa City, Iowa.

Dixon Chief of Police (1917 - 1945) John D. Van Bibber was photographed in this formal portrait after he had been sworn in for service to his community.

J.D. Van Bibber, his wife Clara, and their baby daughter, Gertrude (in the wicker baby buggy), posed for another's camera in front of their West First Street Penny Photo Gallery featuring examples of his photographic art.

DIXON PUBLIC LIBRARY

In 1901, Orris B. Dodge, a successful Dixon industrialist, gave an estimated $20,000 to construct a library building in Dixon to be located at 221 S. Hennepin Avenue. The Dixon Public Library had been established by the Dixon City Council in 1898, making a formal library organization out of the 2,600 volume book collection of the Dixon Hose Company Number One. When the new O.B. Dodge Public Library building was dedicated on February 16, 1901, the *Dixon Evening Telegraph* noted:

> "- - - and yet it must be said that no monetary estimate can be placed on the value of an institute which offers to Dixon one of the finest collections of books of any town in Illinois of comparable size."

During dedication ceremonies, chaired by B.F. Shaw, Dixon's first two librarians, Miss Elizabeth Camp and Miss May F. Wynn, were introduced. In 1902, the Dodge Library received a $15,000 bequest from the estate of Theron Cumins, a business partner of Dodge for many years. The Cumins will was dated May 17, 1898, the same date the City of Dixon established the public library district. The funds were invested and used for the purchase of books over the years. In 1901, approximately 4,000 books were on hand but by 1951 over 30,000 were in circulation. A local history collection was begun in 1922 with the nucleus gifted to the library from the William Barge collection of local history.

The central entrance area of the Dixon Public Library.

The O.B. Dodge Public Library Building contained a large assortment of up-to-date 1901-style equipment when first opened.

Dixon's first livery stable was located on Water (River) Street. This later view of the D.W. McKenney Livery, with an address of 14 West River Street, shows the wear and tear of advancing age. This photograph, taken after the turn-of-the-century, shows the building when it was 65-70 years old.

T.G. Davies' Carriage and Wagon Shop was situated at the southeast corner of West River Street and Hennepin Avenue. The building faced west and was located next to H.V. Fisher's Harness Shop.

This large two-story brick building still stands in downtown Dixon at 105 South Peoria Avenue. It was the location of the Rosbrook and Wasley Livery, with the upper floor being used as a dance hall for many years (note the large double door on the left next to the alley). Two of the firm's rental vehicles, a surrey and a funeral coach, can be seen.

Read and Burright's Livery was located in this West 2nd Street building when this photograph appeared in "A Prospectus of Dixon" in 1910. To the left is the Dixon City Hall.

Shortly after the turn-of-the-century, Charles Rex of rural Sublette traveled to Dixon with his trusted horse, Blue. While in town Mr. Rex purchased this new two-seater carriage and proudly drove it home to show off the latest in vehicle styles of the day. On their way home Mr. Rex and Blue paused to have their picture taken at a local photography studio.

CHARLES REX

Dixon Fire Chief Thomas Coffey, a long time veteran of the local fire department, is shown holding two of the large fire horses. Posed in the middle of a dirt filled West Second Street, Coffey and the equipment-pulling animals are shown with the 1909 Dixon Post Office Building in the right background.

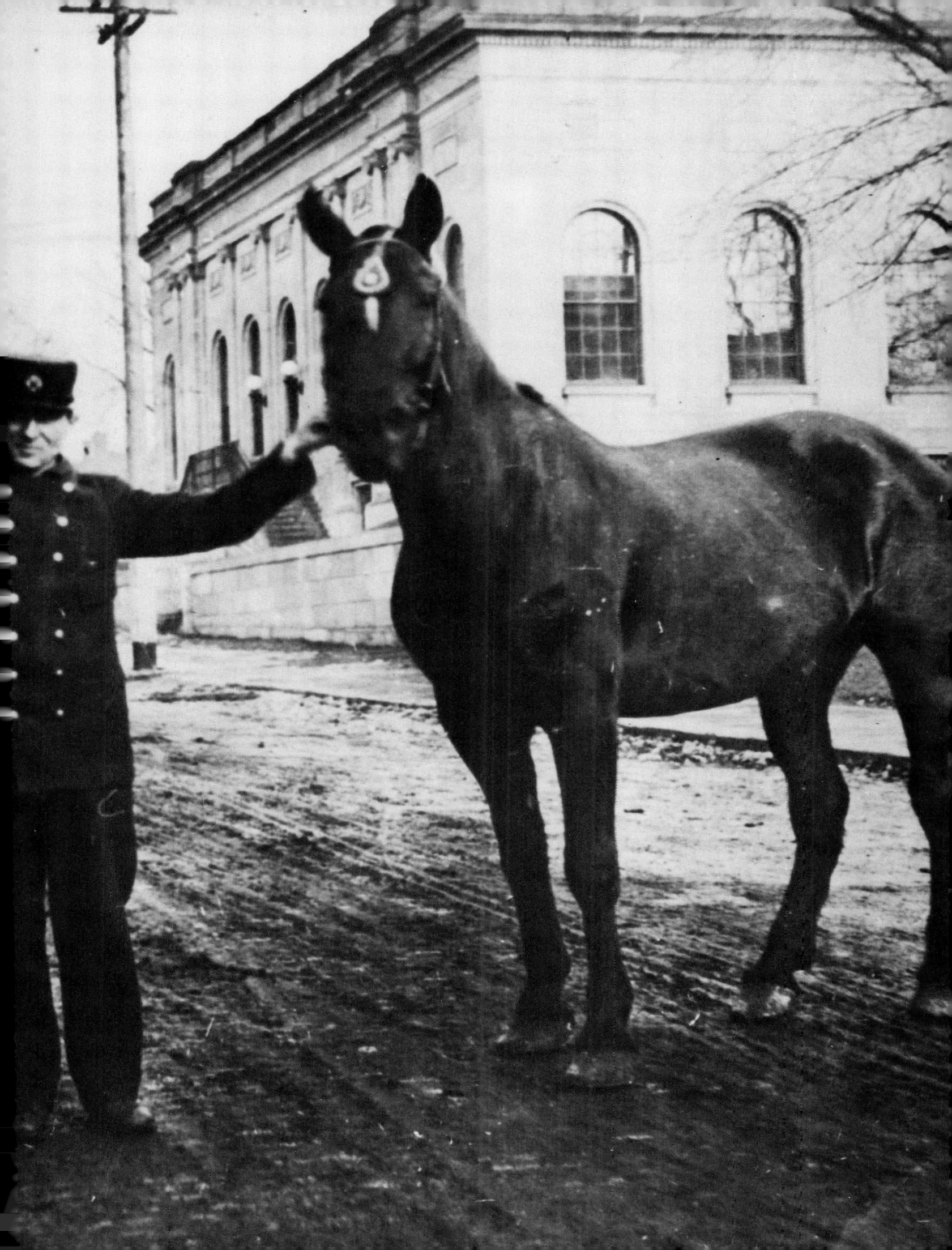

Housed within the Dixon City Hall after 1906, a view of some of the horse stalls and equipment needed for fire fighting are pictured.

Dixon's last two pieces of horse driven equipment, a hook and ladder wagon and pumper, are visible in front of the Dixon City Hall building in 1907.

The Dixon Fire Department's first motor vehicle was purchased in 1913. It was the White truck pictured second from the left in this photograph taken at a later date. The $5,000 truck held a large amount of equipment, carried 1,800 feet of hose, had a self-starter and was capable of speeds up to 70 miles per hour.

NEW CITY HALL

On March 3, 1906, petitions were presented to the members of the Dixon City Council showing that a great number of Dixonites favored the construction of a new city hall. A vote was taken in the community and by a majority of 497 votes it was determined that a new public meeting facility should be built as soon as possible. A contract was awarded in June, 1906 to the local contracting firm of Greig and Baum, who were instructed not to spend more than $30,000 for the entire building. The new city hall included facilities for the fire department, their equipment and their horses as well as administration offices for the police, city engineer, clerks, treasurer plus council rooms and "several other committee rooms." The *Dixon Telegraph* stated that, "the building not only provides for present needs, but contemplates requirements of a much larger city and will therefore be an up-to-date building for half a century or more." At dedication ceremonies held February 22, 1907, a grandson of "Father" John Dixon, Attorney Henry S. Dixon, acted as master of ceremonies for the event and Mayor I.F. Edwards and Attorney A.C. Bardwell made suitable remarks.

The stately Lee County Courthouse, "our own temple of Justice" according to an early issue of the *Dixon Evening Telegraph*, saw cornerstone laying ceremonies conducted on July 1, 1901. The Grecian architecture of the building is distinctive as are all the other elements of the massive edifice centered high on courthouse square in Dixon. Architect for the building was C.E. Brush and William J. McAlpine served as contractor.

LEE COUNTY COURTHOUSE

97

Posed at Attention, these members of Company C, 7th Regiment appear ready to heed the call to battle.

ILLINOIS NATIONAL GUARD

For several years the area north of Dixon along Brinton Avenue now housing the Dixon Correctional Center was referred to as "state grounds." In July of those years the land served as the training fields for several regiments of the Illinois National Guard. In 1915 Camp Dunne (so called to honor then Illinois Governor Dunne) played host to the 2nd, 3rd, 6th and 7th Regiments of the state military organization. Each regiment trained for a full week and usually conducted a parade or gave a band concert in Dixon at the conclusion of their activity. The bandstand in John Dixon Park, the lawn of the Lee County Courthouse and the veranda of the Nachusa House were popular locations for the military band concerts. The opening of "The Colony" in 1918 halted the practice of conducting National Guard camps on the local "state grounds."

While enlisted men of Company A, 2nd Regiment relax, their officers discuss the next phase of their training at Camp Dunne in 1915.

Members of Company B, 6th Regiment, Illinois National Guard are photographed during a training exercise north of Dixon during the summer camp of 1915.

CHARLES WALGREEN

Charles R. Walgreen was born on a farm in Knox County, Illinois, near Galesburg in 1878. His parents, Swedish immigrants, moved their family to Dixon in 1887 where young Walgreen received his early education. He also attended Dixon Business College and worked part-time as an apprentice pharmacist in D.S. Horton's Drug Store on West First Street. Walgreen worked for several Chicago drug stores before enlisting in the Illinois National Guard during the Spanish-American War in 1898. After being discharged, Walgreen became employed in I.W. Blood's drug store at Cottage Grove and Bowen Avenue in Chicago. He later purchased the store, the first of the Walgreen chain of drug stores located across the nation. From 1904 to 1907, he and Ross M. Davis, a native of Polo, owned the Walgreen-Davis Drug Store at 105 West First Street in downtown Dixon. By 1919, he owned 18 stores and ten years later, in 1929, he operated a total of 325. By 1939, the year Walgreen died, the total had reached over 500 drug stores. Charles Walgreen had married Myrtle R. Norton of Normal, Illinois, in 1902 and from that marriage came two children, Charles R., Jr. and Ruth. Walgreen, always interested in aviation, was responsible for the purchase of the first tract of land that would later become the Dixon Municipal Airport. He also served as a Director of the Dixon National Bank, a position his son, also, held for many years. In 1929, he purchased the historic Hazelwood Estate which for years Myrtle Walgreen opened to the public for the benefit of garden clubs of Illinois. The beautiful country estate is now under the management of the University of Illinois. Charles R. Walgreen's contributions to Dixon are numerous with the Walgreen family continuing the interest in Dixon always held by their father.

WILLIAM BRINTON

Born of Quaker stock in 1855 at Greencastle, Indiana, William B. Brinton moved to Illinois in 1865. He was employed as a salesman for the Moline Wagon Company from 1876 to 1893. Brinton served as a United States Marshall for the Southern Illinois District for four years before purchasing an interest in the Peru Plow Company in 1899. He was president of the firm until he moved to Dixon in 1905 where he invested in the Grand Detour Plow Company. Brinton was president of the implement firm for 16 years and Treasurer of the Illinois State Democratic Committee at the same time. The voters of Dixon elected Brinton Major in 1911. While serving as an Illinois State Senator during the 1913-1915 session, Colonel Brinton secured the location of the future Dixon State School in the community. As an initial investor in the Sterling, Dixon and Eastern Railway, he also saw to it that the new state facility was directly served by that transportation system. Brinton and his wife, Rhoda, who he had married in 1875, gave their home at North Crawford Avenue and East Everett Street to the local Masonic organization for use as their Temple in 1926. The people of Dixon renamed the street beside his home North Brinton Avenue in his honor. Colonel William B. Brinton died in Milwaukee on December 20, 1937, at the age of 82.

ANGLO-SWISS

George H. Page, the first white child in Palmyra Township, was born in the log cabin home of his parents in 1834. Before his death in 1899 at the age of 65, Page would become a multi-millionaire and leave a legacy of industrial activity that would affect Dixon for decades to come. After the Civil War, Page joined his brother in Zurich, Switzerland, where he became vice consul for the United State's Department of State. With his brother, he began a process to condense milk and started a small factory in Cham, Switzerland to produce the product. At first, Page sold condensed milk to the U.S. Army and Navy and then to distributors all over Europe. Soon plants were located all through Europe with company headquarters located in London. When tariffs on the company's products threatened to absorb the profits of the export trade to America, Page moved all his operations to New York. In 1888, with William B. Page in charge, George Page started the Ango-Swiss Condensed Milk Company in Dixon. The largest factory of its kind in the world, the $500,000 structure and equipment employed over 250 men and women. No financial bonus was paid to the company to locate in Dixon although the company did ask for assistance in constructing a system of rural macadamized roads with the result that in the first year over 30 miles of hard roads were built. Page laid out the Swissville area of Dixon and brought Swiss workers to Dixon to work in his plant. By 1904 over 150,000 pounds of milk per day from over 10,000 cows, milked daily from area farms, was being received. Farmers received over $40,000 per month from the Borden Company which had purchased the Page operation in 1902.

Each day saw hundreds of farmers delivering milk to the Anglo-Swiss Condensed Milk plant as this circa 1900 photograph shows.

Farmers like Ed Blackburn delivered their milk to the Borden Company in 1910 using a pair of mules to pull the heavy wagons.

Before long, motor vehicles made all deliveries to the Dixon milk producing plant as cars and trucks replaced animals and hard roads became more popular.

An interior view of the huge producing area of the condensed milk plant can be seen in this 1905 photograph.

STERLING, DIXON & EASTERN RAILWAY

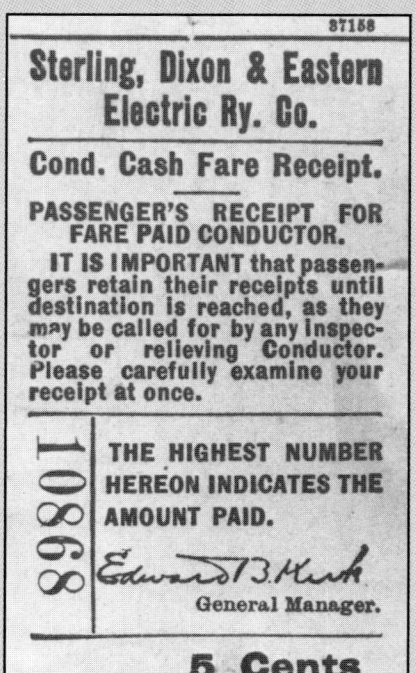

From 1904 to 1925, the Sterling, Dixon and Eastern Railway served its riders well and faithfully only to fall victim to the growing popularity of the automobile. The railway operated as an interurban line between Dixon and Sterling as well as a city streetcar service in both towns for 21 years.

The President of the Milwaukee Transport Company, John I. Beggs, and Henry C. Higgins owned and operated the SD&E from its inception in 1900. Initially, the men were impressed with growth in the two cities and felt a railway system could become profitable.

At the time of the century's change, cars were few, good roads rare, city streets often unpaved and transportation between neighboring cities dependent upon trains, horses or pedestrian pursuits. When interurbans began, public enthusiasm was high, matched only by the later excitement over automobiles.

The SD&E railway was permitted to operated from 6 A.M. to 11 P.M., police and firemen were permitted to ride free when on duty and fares were set at 5¢ for adults and 2½¢ for children. The company was allowed to hang electric wire 18 feet above the city streets and were required to pave its track area when the city paved its streets.

The interurban line between Dixon and Sterling, at first, had three different routes laid out for it. Two of these followed the Rock River on either side while the third route followed closely the route Alternate 30 would take at a later date.

One day in May, 1904, the first car left Dixon at 11 A.M. and arrived in Sterling "in the reasonable time of 25 minutes." Each of the electric cars used cost $8,000, were 50-feet long and 8½-feet wide and would hold 50 to 75 people when necessary.

At first each car had a two-man crew, however this was soon reduced to one man per car acting as both conductor and engineer. Dixon city lines extended north to "The Colony" (in 1915), from Assembly Park along Fellows Street and Palmyra Avenue west and on Galena Avenue to First Street, turning west to College Avenue and the Dementtown area.

From 1920 the company lost money in ever-increasing amounts. A constant drop in customers together with rising costs forced the SD&E railway to cease operations on October 5, 1925. Built at a cost of over $750,000, the railway was later owned by Illinois Northern Utilities with its car barns located at West First Street and Madison Avenue. The offices of the line were contained in Colonel John Dement's old home that also served as a waiting room.

Over 10,000 feet of 60-70 pound iron street car tracks were taken up from the streets of Dixon in 1934 and used, along with truck loads of heavy paving bricks, to build the Dixon Airport hangar. The streetcars were sold along with other railway equipment over the years. The dream of the SD&E to provide interurban and city customers with streetcar transportation was at an end.

In the winter of 1905-1906, Drew's Coal Company did their best to entice customers to purchase their winter's supply of heating coal from them. W.D. Drew was one of the first merchants in Dixon to install two telephones; one from the Dixon Home Telephone Company, the other from the Central Union Telegraph Company that had started telephone service in Dixon in 1904.

W.D. DREW COAL COMPANY

W.D. Drew operated his coal yard business at 90 South Peoria Avenue for many years after the turn-of-the-century. Mr. and Mrs. Drew posed proudly for the photographer in front of their small office building. Drew's truck scale can be seen through the building's front window.

MILLER GARAGE

The J.E. Miller Garage in 1910 was located at 214-216 East First Street in Dixon. Having their picture taken was Harry Hintz, Oscar Johnson, Joe Miller, Claude Horton (behind the wheel) and an unidentified customer of the Miller Garage.

ARCHITECTURE

Examples of many early styles of architecture, including Queen Anne, Victorian, Greek Revival, Italiante Victorian, Bysantine and Victorian Gothic may be seen during a walk along Dixon's quiet tree-lined streets. Many of her finer homes have passed from view in the name of progress but a selection remains to give the viewer an idea of how Dixon looked in years gone by.

The residence of E.W. Smith in 1896, this home is now the property of Mr. and Mrs. James E. Dixon. It's current address is 521 S. Peoria Ave.

Located on Artesian Place near the corner of East River Street, this home was the Salzman Family residence for many years. It is a find example of a late 1890's frame one-story family home that was well used and well loved. The home is no longer to be seen.

The large multi-roomed residence of Theron Cumins was located on North Galena Avenue. Torn down in the 1970's, the Victorian Gothic style home was replaced by the First Federal Savings and Loan Association building, 413 N. Galena Avenue.

In 1896, this was the three-story home of John V. Thomas and his family. Thomas, a successful insurance agent in the city, was also a popular political figure for many years. Today, the home is owned by Mr. and Mrs. Edward D. Evett and its current address is 507 E. Everett St.

It may be said that Dixon is one of the prettiest cities of its size in the West. It is typically a New England city, situated on the bank of the Rock River, the "Hudson of the West", surrounded by wooded hills, traversed by well shaded streets and avenues, and the center of one of the most beautiful farming sections in Illinois. In either direction along the river and especially up-stream, is to be found scenery of picturesqueness and beauty, rarely seen in a prairie country.

The streets of the city are always in good condition. All the principal thoroughfares are macadamized, and the disagreeable mud, so common in a prairie country, is never seen.

Each summer the carpenters and masons are very busy building residences in every part of the city. There is no evidence of a decline and all lines of business are prospering.

From The Souvenior of Dixon
Published by Dana C. Johnson
1896

Built by Alanzo H. Tillison, a Dixon druggist, this large frame home was sold in 1903 to G.H.T. Shaw. Later, it was sold to R.R. Frye who, in 1910, sold it to Horace G. Reynolds. Reynolds added to the home and remodeled it extensively. Now the location of the Dixon Dells Apartments, the beautiful home carried an address of East Morgan Street and North Galena Avenue.

In 1896 the residence of Charles H. Hughes, this prime example of a double porch home is located at the corner of East Boyd Street and North Galena Avenue. It is now the residence of Mr. and Mrs. Forrest J. Trautwein and carries an address of 105 East Boyd Street.

PRATT-REED GROCERY

Kirby J. Reed operated a grocery store in Dixon for many years. The store was at first located at 91 Galena Avenue on the south side of Commerical Alley. K.J. Reed can be seen on the left in the photo.

The Pratt-Reed Grocery was a very promotion-minded retail store. In this photo can be seen K.J. Reed and Vernon Tennant behind a display of the Richelieu brand food products. In addition, the West First Street grocery was the first retail grocery in Dixon to handle fresh cut meats; a move that was long lamented by every butcher and butcher shop in town at the time.

In 1917, Reed and his partner, Frank M. Pratt, started the Pratt-Reed Grocery at 116 West First Street using the advertising slogan "The Best Of Everything In Our Line." From the left in the photo are: Andrew Meyers, clerk; Frank M. Pratt, partner; an unknown customer; Irene Nelson, bookkeeper and cashier; and Kirby J. Reed, partner.

BEIER'S BAKERY

Beier's Bakery, whose advertising slogan "Baked Fine Since '69" is remembered with fondness, was a major local employer for many years. Rheinhold Beier settled in Dixon after leaving Erfort, Germany, and in 1869, established his own bakery in Dementtown. Beier turned out 40 loaves of bread on his first day in business.

From the first, Beier considered a quality product, honestly made and sold, to be his business credo. The business expanded greatly over the years until, in 1877, a new bakery was constructed. Beier operated a retail store at 126 West First Street and the beginnings of a delivery route business.

In 1895, the second generation of Beiers, William and Otto, entered the business as it continued to grow and prosper. Soon Rheinhold Beier retired and in 1906, Otto Beier purchased his brother's share of the firm. By 1899, Beier's Bakery had outgrown their First Street location and had erected a new building at 107 Hennepin Avenue. The bakery's business continued to expand until, in 1923, yet another larger building was constructed.

George H. Beier, Otto's son, joined his father in 1925 and continued to head the company until his death in the 1960's. Beier's new plant was located on River Street and Ottawa Avenue in 1939. It served for 23 years as a modern prototype of a complete bakery operation.

The local bakery ceased production in 1962. With the closing of the bakery, the familiar orange and white covered loaves of Beier's Bread were to be seen no longer.

The 60th Anniversary of Beier's Bakery was celebrated in 1929 with this huge decorated birthday cake.

The Beier Bakery, in 1877, was next located at 126 West First Street in downtown Dixon. A full line bakery and grocery store was operated by Otto Beier.

Beier's "Golden Sunlight Bakery," at the time of its construction in 1939, was considered the most advanced bakery of its kind in the middle west. Located on East River Street and Ottawa Avenue, the plant produced Beier's products until the bakery closed in 1962.

The original Rheinhold Beier Bakery was located here in 1869. The frame building still stands at the corner of West 6th Street and Depot Avenue.

Henry Chamnesss, a longtime baker with Beier's Bakery, is shown operating the dough-making machine in June, 1937.

In 1899, Beier's Bakery moved to larger quarters at 107 Hennepin Avenue. This photogaph, taken October, 1927, shows the bread company's delivery trucks and salesmen.

Leon Hart, co-owner, on the right and George Nettz, his partner, casually pose for the camera man in front of their Auburn-Ford dealership. Notice the "Free Air" sign on the window and the carriage parked in front of the garage to the right.

GEORGE NETTZ COMPANY

George Nettz became a Ford automobile dealer in 1906 when he opened a garage and sales room in a former livery stable. The frame building located on West First Street is today the site of the Hey Brothers Ice Cream building. The garage was moved in 1908 to East First Street. In the fall of 1911 Nettz moved to 113-115 East First Street where he resided until 1920 when his garage was moved next door to the Elks Club on Ottawa Avenue.

Posed proudly in his Ford car George Nettz shows off his 1911 automobile with its hard rubber tires, hand-cranked starter, brass running lamps, convertible top and left-hand drive.

The George Nettz Company handled a complete line of Fordson Tractors and farm equipment.

Francis Haynes parked the Willard Service Station truck owned by George Nettz on a city street so this photograph could be taken in 1912. Note the chain attached to the rear tires for added traction while driving on the mud roads.

The eleven Nettz Garage employees are shown in the repair shop of the firm in 1914.

DIXON STATE COLONY

UNDER CONSTRUCTION

WORKERS POSE FOR PHOTO

Illinois State Senator William B. Brinton of Dixon was an active advocate of the establishment of the "Illinois Colony for Curable Epileptics" in the community during the legislative session of 1913-14. Construction work began on the main building in the spring of 1916, but was delayed many times due to labor shortages, strikes and assorted difficulties caused by World War I. The large facility, located on approximately 1,100 acres along the Rock River on Dixon's far northeastern side, was considered to be prime land for the institution. In May, 1918, the Colony opened with 50 residents and a hospital staff of 16. By the end of the first summer, 400 permanent residents lived on the grounds. The name of the main road in front of the facility was changed from North Crawford Avenue to North Brinton Avenue in honor of Colonel Brinton and as time went by an extension of the Sterling, Dixon and Eastern Electric Railway line was built to the main gates of the state hospital. A peak resident population of over 5,500 was reached in the 1960's when the title of Dixon Developmental Center was used for the institution. Changes in mental health programs resulted in the closing of the state operated hospital in the 1980's.

HOME LUMBER & COAL COMPANY

In 1923, when this photograph was taken, the owner of the Home Lumber and Coal Company was Dement Schuler. Until 1955, when the delivery of coal ceased, the Home Lumber Company handled the heating fuel in several grades and sizes. Pictured in the firm's office, from left to right, are: Schuler, Albert Frerichs, coal deliveryman, and Esther J. Whitcombe, bookkeeper.

DIXON HOTEL

W.A. Schuler constructed the Dixon Inn, later known as the Dixon Hotel, in 1909-1910, at the corner of West First Street and Highland Avenue. Harry Bailey was the popular lodging facility's first manager when it opened October 3, 1910. Consisting of 32 rooms with two or three bathrooms on each floor and hot and cold water in each room, the Dixon Inn soon was operating at full capacity. The building later underwent a remodeling that reduced its size to half. The Dixon Hotel was demolished in the mid-1970's after having been an active part of Dixon for over 60 years.

Y.M.C.A.

Y. M. C. A. Building, Dixon, Ill.

The beginning of the Dixon YMCA occurred 28 years after a young dry goods clerk named George Williams gathered 11 young men together in London, England to begin the YMCA organization. The Dixon branch began November 25, 1872 in the offices of Jason C. Ayers in the Exchange Block on Dixon's Galena Avenue. Twenty-three young Dixonites responded to a published notice in the *Dixon Telegraph and Herald.* The local Y continued to grow and become an integral part of Dixon community life. By 1901, the local Y played host to the 29th Illinois State Convention of the YMCA and began seriously to consider the construction of their own building facility. At the time, activities were centered in the Ellias Bovey Building at the southeast corner of East First Street and Ottawa Avenue in downtown Dixon. During 1904, as a result of a 36-day revival in Dixon by Reverend Billy Sunday, over $8,000 was raised for a permanent Dixon YMCA home. A later full-fledged fund raising drive allowed the organization to acquire property at the northwest corner of South Galena Avenue and West Third Street on which to build a fully-equipped, debt-free building. The Y Building was dedicated June, 1907, and served the community until March 15, 1929, when it was closed and torn down to make way for a gas station. For all practical purposes, the YMCA in Dixon ended at this time for a period of 31 years until 1960 when it was once again activated.

The E.H. Rickard home overlooked John Dixon Park and was considered a prime example of a Victorian frame house of the era. Ornate decorations, many large windows and a spacious front porch in addition to a full basement and attic gave the many rooms the house contained a well balanced and lived-in look. Mr. and Mrs. Rickard enjoyed their place of residence and were proud to pose for a family photographer in their favorite chairs. The Rickard's next door neighbor, C.P. Williams, maintained a gracious home (shown at left) that in appearance was almost a duplicate of theirs. Both these find old homes continue to stand proudly just a half block off North Galena Avenue on Morgan Street.

DIXON COUNTRY CLUB

At first called the Dixon Golf Club when started in 1918, the organization used an 80 acre tract of land between Lowell Park Road and North Crawford (later North Brinton Avenue) for their activities. In 1927, the land was purchased for $22,500. In the nine-year interval, the Dixon Country Club was formed and expended about $18,000 on land and building improvements. Later additions to the club included a swimming pool area, enlargements and improvements to the club house facilities and increased facilities for parking and storing of golf related equipment.

The Dixon Knights of Columbus was organized in 1902 with John E. Ford serving as their first Grand Knight. The organization of Catholic men met on the third floor of the Opera House building until 1905. Locations after that date include rented rooms in the Brown Building, Vaile Building and later, in club rooms on East First Street over Duffy's Garage. The Knights of Columbus purchased their first home at 506 West Third Street in 1926 at a cost of $40,000. Dedication for the new Knights of Columbus building was held February 8, 1958; the facility that continues today to serve Council 690 of the Dixon Knights of Columbus.

KNIGHTS OF COLUMBUS

This aerial view of the Dementtown business district shows the western district of Dixon when it was a busy and vibrant place. Long the center of railroad activity in the community, Dementtown's business enterprises consisted of mills, depots, groceries, taverns and all manner of other business activities.

DEMENTTOWN

In 1918-19 these family photographs were taken in the Dementtown area and placed in the family album now owned by Mrs. Edward Sorbe. Seen by the general public for the first time, they serve to remind us of the "good old days" in Dementtown 70 years ago.

A photograph taken from the roof of the Nachusa House shows the still smoldering fire that destroyed the 1876 Dixon Opera House.

OPERA HOUSE FIRE

The Dixon Opera House opened on a cool fall evening in 1876. For the next 27 years, the entertainment center of Dixon flourished on the city's busy Galena Avenue. The beautiful Opera House was a credit to the community and the focal point for countless events for its more than 25 years of service. By June, 1903, however, it was merely a smoke blackened hull of its former self after the ravages of a raging fire destroyed all but the outer walls of the once proud and grand edifice. The inferno caused over $40,000 in damages, took in excess of 14,000 barrels of water to put out the fire and occupied the efforts of every volunteer fireman in the city. The Opera House was rebuilt by contractor William J. McAlpine with amazing speed, re-opening again to over 1,000 guests at a November 17, 1903 comedy performance of *When Johnny Comes Marching Home*. The Opera House's second fire took place on February 18, 1920 causing over $100,000 in damages. Total interior destruction took place in this fire which left only charred ruins and smoking ashes in its wake. L.G. Rorer, manager of the Family Theatre at that time, formed a corporation to rebuild the structure. McAlpine was once again the contractor. In 1922, the Dixon Theatre emerged from the ashes to serve the public as the city's largest motion picture palace for over 60 years.

Pictured are the remains of the Dixon Opera House, with the Rickard and Emerson buildings seen to the right, after a $100,000 fire on February 18, 1920.

THE DIXON THEATRE

Part of a large crowd waiting outside the Dixon Theatre can be seen in this 1920's postcard view. In its first years, the theatre presented six acts of vaudeville, a seven-piece orchestra and a silent movie for a general admission price of $1.00. Until the 1980's, when its screen fell silent and its future was clouded in doubt, the Dixon Theatre played host to countless thousands of movie attending audiences.

Another popular theatre, the Lee Theatre, located on East First Street, was built in 1936 by the Lindquist Construction Company of St. Charles, Illinois. It opened with suitable fanfare on November 14th of that year and advertised itself to be "one of the first theatres in the world built for perfect sound, perfect vision and perfect air conditioning."

In 1965, after 29 years of nightly movies, the Lee Theatre closed and was replaced by an Osco Drug Store.

The Dixon Theatre, opened on March 15, 1922 amid great fanfare, was the pride and joy of Dixon for many years. L.G. Rorer, president of the company operating the motion picture house which had cost over $200,000 to construct and furnish, referred to it as "the Theatre Beautiful" in his advertisements. Lavish decorative accessories, spacious seating, synchronized sound for live musical presentations, and a full range of silent movies and vaudeville presentations marked the Dixon Theatre. The first movie with sound played on June 14, 1929, while the organ which accompanied silent films was heard for the last time on May 30, 1936. These unusual interior pictures of the Dixon Theatre were from an early post card.

E.J. FERGUSON HARDWARE STORE

The E.J. Ferguson Hardware Store, a longtime Dixon retail business endeavor, was located in the Masonic Building at the southwest corner of West First Street and Peoria Avenue.

The Great Majestic Range was a popular item at Ferguson's and occupied a large amount of the available floor space.

Nine employees of Ferguson's Hardware staff posed for the cameraman in 1917.

CHRISTIAN CHURCH

The first home of the Christian Church in Dixon was in the Bovey Building at the corner of East First Street and Ottawa Avenue in the 1890's. In 1921, the church organization purchased the building of the First Universalist Society of Dixon located on Hennepin Avenue and West Second Street. On March 16, 1947, a terrible fire almost totally consumed the beautiful natural limestone edifice. After two years of rebuilding, the church was rededicated on June 19, 1949 completely free of debt. While living in Dixon from 1920 to 1932, Nell Reagan and her sons Neil and Ronald attended services at the Christian Church and participated in its Sunday School activities.

ST. ANNE'S CATHOLIC CHURCH

St. Anne's Catholic Church was constructed at a cost of $55,000 in 1928-29 on East Morgan Street in Dixon. The northside Catholic community, consisting of 80 families and 250 people, welcomed the dedication of the church on July 28, 1929.

The first attempt to organize a church for the black population of Dixon resulted in a frame dwelling being built on Hennepin Avenue between Second and Third Streets. Only a Sunday School survived these efforts and it wasn't until 1915 that an attempt to organize a regular church membership and continue the Sunday School was made. Church meetings were held first at 606 Monroe Avenue and later, at 516 West Sixth Street. The church, then known as the Community Church, was pastored by a Reverend Fletcher, a Baptist minister. In 1916, young people of the church started a fund-raising campaign to build a new church. When this effort had accumulated $300, a building lot was purchased at 605 Madison Avenue. It wasn't until 1920, however, that Clara Thomas successfully promoted the idea of constructing a church building on the lot. The first 18 bricks for the new building were purchased by holding a "Brick Party" at which bricks were sold for $1.00 each. Under the direction of Reverend and Mrs. Hawkins, the church building was completed. The congregation later moved into a church building at the corner of West Third Street and Madison Avenue. Here Dixon's Second Baptist Church continues to serve its members.

SECOND BAPTIST CHURCH

"Slipping" boulders from the Castle Rock cut in order to construct Illinois Route 2 north of Dixon needed the assistance of motor, man and beast. As this picture records, on January 16, 1924, the very roads that carried the vehicles that marked the end of the use of horses as major transportation were built using the services of the sturdy animals.

The mud condition of Illinois Route 2 near Dixon can readily be seen in this March 1, 1924 photograph. Bill Balen and Ed Campbell, employees of the Illinois Department of Transportation, are pictured next to their narrow-tired automobile.

In June, 1924, work on Illinois Route 2 north of Dixon was progressing rapidly as this photograph shows. The rock cut at Wernicke's Hill is seen under construction using steam and horsepower.

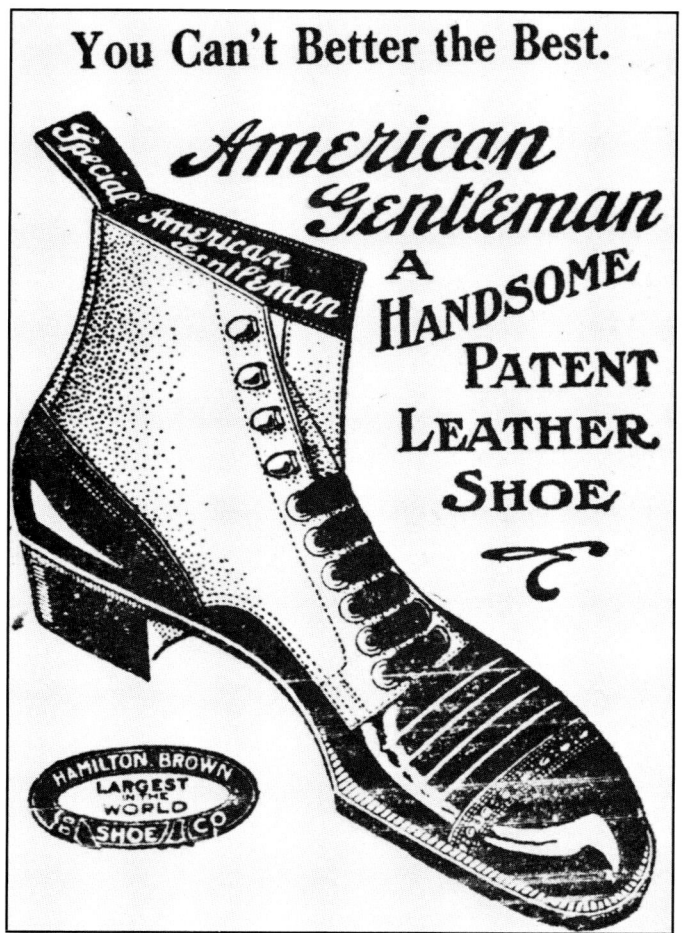

This post card view of the Watson-Plummer Shoe Company plant in Dixon also shows the "Little Shop" factory to the rear.

The West First Street plant of the Watson-Plummer Shoe Company was one of Dixon's largest employers. Here were made the nationally famous "Red School House Shoes" and many other famous brands of shoes for both men and women. This post card view of the company's two plants was used as an advertising device for many years.

SHOE BUSINESS

For almost a quarter of a century, the shoe making industry in Dixon was profitable both for its owners and for a major part of the local industrial scene. The Fargo Shoe Company building and land was sold to the Roger Company in 1910 with that site later being occupied by the Reynolds Wire Company and later, by Beier and Company.

In 1902, Frank Watson formed the Watson-Plummer Shoe Company and bought the Henderson Shoe Company's building and assets. Production of children's shoes under the name "The Little Red School House Shoe Company" was begun almost immediately. For the next 11 years, until 1913, Watson ran the shoe company in Dixon. His death at this time caused the Brown Shoe Company of St. Louis to purchase the local shoe concern.

In the 1920's, the "Little Shop" factory, east of the main building on West First Street was razed and a baseball field was developed on this site. Here the Dixon Brown's and other local baseball teams played each summer.

After converting the old shoemaking apparatus to newer, more modern, equipment, shoe production rose to over 2,500 pairs of high grade women's shoes per day. In excess of $50,000 was spent making improvements on the Brown Shoe Company building in the early 1920's.

The early 1930's saw work stoppages occur with increasing frequency until, in March, 1933, the economic condition of the Depression forced a complete closing of the shoemaking industry in Dixon.

In 1934, the introduction of cloth shoe production once again opened the shoe factory. Leather shoe production was also started. At this time hourly wages were introduced; men receiving 27½¢ per hour and women 25¢ per hour for a 40-hour work week.

The Freeman Shoe Company, in 1937, announced plans to open a Dixon plant in the old 1893 knitting factory building on Lincoln Avenue that had formerly been the home of the American Wagon Factory. After two years in Dixon, following the firm's purchase of the Brown Shoe Company plant in 1939, the Freeman Shoe Company became the sole shoe manufacturing company in the community.

The Brown Shoe Company plant in Dixon was an imposing four-story structure that turned out millions of pairs of shoes over the years.

In 1915, workmen were photographed doing reconstruction work at the Brown Shoe Company plant on West First Street.

The North Dixon High School was erected in 1868-69 at a total cost of $20,000. It stood on the site of what is now Heritage Square on Dixon's north side. After the construction of the new Dixon High School in 1928-29, the school was used as a grade school until taken down for Heritage Square in the late 1960's.

The White Brick School or South Side High School was built on the southwest corner of 5th Street and Hennepin Avenue in 1887. Its original cost was $5,500. In 1892-93 it was enlarged at a cost of $17,000 and was destroyed by fire in 1907. This school was replaced at that time by what is now known as South Central School.

The 1893 graduating class of the North Dixon High School was photographed in formal clothing for their official class picture. The graduates were Mabel Kaye, Mae Strohm, Elizabeth Buckaloo, Eva M. Cook, Ethel Halstead, Agnes A. Coffey and Besse C. Pankhurst. Lester G. Street is the lone boy shown in the picture as Adam McKenny graduated but did not have his picture taken with the Class of '93.

This South Central Grade School class posed at strict attention for this class picture. Taken in 1910, it shows the first grade class of 14 girls and 12 boys.

RONALD REAGAN

Born on February 6, 1911, Ronald Reagan's birthplace was a five-room flat over a bakery on Main Street in Tampico, Illinois. A ten-pound baby at birth, he was immediately nicknamed by his father, Jack, who said, "For such a little bit of a fat Dutchman, he makes an awful lot of noise, doesn't he?" Two-year-old Neil, his brother, refused to look at the new baby as he had been promised a sister.

Reagan was nine when his father was offered a job in Dixon at the Fashion Boot Store. The family moved into a white frame house in Dixon at 816 South Hennepin Avenue where they lived until 1924. When ten years old, "Dutch" Reagan worked as a caddy at the Dixon Country Club and by the time he was 15 he had a job as a lifeguard. The Lowell Park swimming beach was a popular summer place that saw Reagan earn $18 per week and all the nickel root beers and ten cent hamburgers he could eat. He is credited with saving 77 lives while spending seven summers as a lifeguard on the Rock River.

Reagan attended North Dixon High School on Morgan Street from 1924 to 1928. He was active in school politics and dramatics. His passion was football despite his 5'3", 108-pound frame. In his senior year, popular "Dutch" Reagan was elected president of the high school student body.

Following graduation, he attended Eureka College near Peoria. After graduation from college with a degree in economics, Reagan worked in broadcast radio until his movie career began in 1938.

High school class photo - 1928

The 1927-28 high school football team. Reagan is in the front row, second from right.

Reagan was the Drum Major of the Dixon Y.M.C.A. Marching Band. He is shown with his marching baton at far left in the photo.

On duty at Lowell Beach. Reagan is sitting in a swimsuit on the platform.

"Dutch" as a life guard at Lowell Beach Park.

DIXON HIGH SCHOOL

Constructed at a cost of over $580,000 and dedicated on December 13, 1929, ten years after the 1919 consolidation of the Northside and Southside High Schools, the Dixon High School continues even yet today to be one of the most beautiful schools of its kind in the middle west. Voters had approved the concept of the new school on June 18, 1927, and passed two bond issues to finance it in 1927 and 1928. When opened, the high school did not have the use of the cafeteria (then located on the third floor) nor the auditorium. Constructed on the north side of the Rock River on an area that had at one time been called Pleasure Park, a horse racing area, the school's auditorium was not completed until 1935 when work was financed in part by Federal WPA funds.

The five gentlemen of the 1930 Centennial Committee planned a wide variety of activities to celebrate Dixon's Centennial. From the left they are: Charles Miller (Committee Chairman), vice president of Boyton-Richards Company; Louis Pitcher, manager of Home Telephone Company and president of the Dixon Park Board; George C. Dixon, Illinois State Representative; J. Barry Lennon, vice president of Dixon National Bank; and Dement Schuler, president of Home Lumber and Coal Company.

CHAPTER IV

CHANGING YEARS

1930 - 1959

The centennial of the founding of Dixon was a subject of constant conversation in 1930. The residents of the community celebrated the event to the best of their collective abilities with the dedication of an airport, a bridge and a statue plus many other activities.

In the first year of the 30's, Boyd Casket Company came to town to open a new factory while The Bowman Brothers Shoe Store, the Edna Mattress Shop ("Dixon's Fashion Corner") and the A & P Grocery with Roy Eastman as manager, started a downtown business.

In 1932 Hal Roberts began a wholesale beer distribution business at 80 Galena Avenue while Carl and Betty Peterson opened the Rainbow Inn. The Grand Detour Plow Works, which had been purchased in 1919 by the I.J. Case Company, closed that year. This action ended the long plow-making industry connection with the community.

Reynolds Field, a 1932 Christmas present to the city, was a memorial to Horace G. Reynolds given by his daughters. Dixon received an $11,000 grant from the Federal government to improve the field. Government assistance was also received so that 130 men went to work on various state highway projects while an additional 35 men were employed by the city at $5 per day to take up the old street car tracks and paving blocks around the community. These federally funded projects helped end "days of idleness, nights of worry" so common during the time.

A Montgomery Ward retail store opened in Dixon in 1934 and Charles K. Willett began a consulting engineering firm at this time. Oscar Johnson opened a Buick automobile garage on North Galena Avenue while B.W. Harrison started business as a Chevrolet automobile dealer at 414 West First Street in 1935.

In 1936, the election of Courtney Ryan as the first President of the Dixon Jaycees marked the beginning of an outstanding organization in the community. Dixon police and fire personnel received a 7% wage increase in 1936 and remembered well that they had taken a 10% wage deduction just short months before.

Advertising the slogan "DIXON SOLES KEEP AMERICA ON ITS FEET," Dixon's Cut Sole Company was organized in 1937 with 105 employees. On September 27, 1937, Ronald "Dutch" Reagan's first motion picture, *Love Is On The Air*, was shown by L.G. Rorer at his Lee Theatre which had been built the year before by the Lindquist Construction Company of St. Charles and Dixon.

When Willard E. Beanblossom came to Dixon in the middle 1930's he took over the Laing Feed Service on West River Street next door to another long-time Dixon business, Sinow and Wieman, Inc. Frank L. Randall started Chapel Hill on Dixon's north side in 1938. In this year, too, the Lawton Brothers of Palmyra Township began home delivery of milk in Dixon and three years later started a cheese and dressed poultry store at 315 West First Street.

The dedication of the Loveland Community House gave Dixon one of the finest such facilities in the mid-west. Other dedications in 1939 included those for the newly constructed Abraham Lincoln Bridge and the Illinois National Guard Armory. This year, too, marked the start of the Huffman family tradition in the gas business.

By December 7, 1941, the "day that would live in infamy," Dixon's Civil Defense Council had been organized. In 1942 the first local blackout took place. The Green River Ordinance Plant south of Dixon opened and produced, among other weapons, a 4,000 pound blockbuster bomb that was declared to be "awful" by all who saw it.

War time efforts on the homefront in Dixon included a "Dogs for Defense" program, a Marine Corps knife collecting effort, and scrap iron, paper, waste fat and rubber collection activities to help the war effort. In July, 1943, a "V Day" program at Lowell Park attracted 10,000 people to "let off pressure of war time jitters" with an old fashioned picnic and a full day of happy activities.

In January, 1943, a $100,000 fire destroyed the F.W. Woolworth store at 114 West First Street in downtown Dixon and the Brown Shingle Restaurant began a long-time tenure in the food and beverage business. By 1944, the year the C. Marshall Oldsmobile dealership began, there were 1,400 Dixon men and women in the armed services of their country.

The May 7th end of the war in Europe followed on September 2, 1944, with a VJ Day celebration of the end of the war with Japan brought joy and happiness to Dixon. This was the year Rock River Ready Mix began operations and Venier's Jewelry Store opened on West First Street.

Matt and Chester Goral started a roofing company in Dixon and Joseph and Victor Eichler's new West First Street store opened for business on March 17, 1946. In this same year Shippert's Moving and Storage Company along with Eller and Willey Block Company entered the business world.

1948 saw the establishment of the Dixon Rotary Club with Harry Kerz heading the 23 man organization as its first president while Melvin Murphy took over the operation of a small grocery store at 791 Brinton Avenue. The Raynor Manufacturing Company, makers of overhead garage doors, moved to Dixon from Quincy, Illinois, when their newly built brick building was completed in 1948.

The Henry Pratt Company came to Dixon in 1949 to locate in the former Grand Detour Plow Works building. WSDR Radio began operations in this year and were able to fully report the Thanksgiving Eve fire that destroyed the historic Auditorium in Assembly Park known as "The Dome" for many years.

In June, 1950, the final work on Dixon's $259,000 Memorial Pool was completed. Crowds of Dixonites viewed the $100,000 fire at Klines Department Store on November 8, 1950, just months after the August Injun Summer Days celebration was completed. Dixon's hometown movie actor, Ronald "Dutch" Reagan, was a special guest at the fun-filled fall event.

E.L. "Babe" Fazzi had been in the retail television business for a year at 317 East First Street when Brooks Drug Store moved to a new location in downtown Dixon. At this time a Buick Special, 2-door, 6-passenger, automobile could be purchased from Zien Buick, 108 North Galena Avenue, for $2,016.65. Also in this year, 1951, W. David Ames purchased the Ralph Salzman Building at 118 East First Street to begin the Ames Furniture Company.

The Illinois Conference of the Seventh Day Adventists purchased the 60 acre Reynoldswood Estate and its 25 room mansion for a Youth Camp in April of 1952. The local J.C. Penney Store, which had opened in Dixon in 1921 with Sam Stanfield as its first manager, celebrated the Golden Anniversary of the Penney organization in 1952. The Dixon Elks Club, too, celebrated their 50th birthday under the leadership of Elwin Glessner.

A pair of car dealerships opened in Dixon in 1953: Dixon Motors and Herzog Mercury Sales. The Edwards Clinic at 7th Street and Galena Avenue was begun in the same year that saw the July 10th Grand Opening of the newly restored Nachusa House.

The Assembly Park area was annexed to Dixon in 1954; the largest land addition to the city since 1896. A disastrous fire in December of the year destroyed the Kavanaugh Plastic Company in Dementtown and caused great damage to the Henry Pratt Company next door. In the following year Washington School was constructed and in June of 1955 the USF&G Insurance firm moved into their north side building facing the Rock River.

The City of Dixon, in December, 1956, bought the Dixon Water Company for $800,000 and the Bordan Starlac Dry Milk facilities were moved to Dixon that year. Dixon's population was determined to be 18,851 in 1957, a figure that included residents of the Dixon State School and Swissville area for the first time. The Illinois Grange held a convention in Dixon that summer while the first edition of "Nachusa House News" appeared in the page of the Dixon Evening Telegraph.

A million dollar fire destroyed the South College Avenue plant of the Dixon Publishing Company on February 16, 1958, the Community Chest raised $30,000 for community organizations and the Lee County Board of Supervisors asked voters to approve a $300,000 three-story addition to the county court house to hold a new jail and county offices. County voters soundly defeated the proposal.

As the 1950's ended, Dixonites saw a ban against parking on Galena Avenue take place, pinball machines outlawed in the community and the move to new Peoria Avenue facilities by the *Dixon Evening Telegraph* after a 65-year stay on East First Street. Dixon Commercial Electric and Clayton's Flowers both began business in Dixon in 1959. The A.H. Lancaster Gym was dedicated at the Dixon High School on the night of November 27, 1959, in honor of the long time Dixon public school principal and superintendent.

In addition to a River Street carnival (photo), Dixonites were treated to a long series of events celebrating Dixon's Centennial in the fall of 1930. An essay contest was conducted by the public schools of Dixon which was won by Dorothy Hoyle, a 9th grade student at E.C. Smith School. Her teacher was Miss Esther Barton. The high school winner was Ruth Carner, sophomore, whose teacher was Miss Enroth. Miss Hoyle and Miss Carner each received $3 for their winning essays on Dixon's history.

DIXON'S CENTENNIAL

The City of Dixon celebrated its 100th anniversary during September 21-24, 1930, with what was then termed "the grandest pageant in its history." Events in the Centennial celebration marking Dixon's birthday included ceremonies dedicating the city's municipal airport, the new $166,000 Peoria Avenue bridge and a bronze statue of young Abe Lincoln on the site of the old blockhouse in North Dixon where the future President had served as a soldier in the Black Hawk War of 1832.

The ceremonies marking the culmination of the three projects, two of which had been planned or projected for more than a decade, were happy coincidences which went together well.

The three accomplishments dedicated during the Centennial were symbolic of the 100-year span of the city's history. The Lincoln statue of a young soldier reminded all of Dixon's beginnings as a frontier community; the bridge was the ultimate symbol of the successful conquest of the Rock River; and the airport was the promise of a new age ahead which all knew would revolutionize civilization.

A huge parade was held with over 50 floats, a large group of Winnebago Indians set up a camp and village on the high school athletic fields to remind everyone of the early Indian influences on the area and over three score airplanes took part in an all day aerial show at the city's new airport. The Peoria Avenue Bridge was the scene of a large street dance the night following its dedication by Illinois Governor Louis Emerson. An overflow crowd attended the Lincoln statue dedication with George C. Dixon, great grandson of "Father" John Dixon presiding. A balloon performance by Professor Andy Owen of Dixon, "the world's only one-armed balloonist," and a fireworks display over the Rock River concluded the three day event.

CRUNELLE STATUE

This rare photograph shows the Lincoln Statue made by artist and sculptor Leonard Crunelle who is shown next to it. A 23-year-old Abraham Lincoln, then a Captain of Volunteers during the Black Hawk War of 1832, is shown as a larger-than-life bronze statue. Crunelle began work on the statue in February, 1930 and was present when it was dedicated in the fall of that year during Dixon's Centennial celebration. The statue is cast in bronze and rests on a 6½-foot high base of solid Georgia granite. The young Lincoln in the statue is 10-feet high with a 2½-foot concrete base under the granite pedestal. The total height of the statue is more than 19-feet above ground level.

A large overflow crowd assembled on the grounds of the Fort Dixon blockhouse on September 23, 1930 to view the unveiling and dedication of the Lincoln Statue. This unusual view shows a covered statue with the Dixon business district in the background across the Rock River.

When the famous coast-to-coast Lincoln Highway was being planned shortly before the start of World War I, it was discovered that there were two places along the entire length of the highway that Lincoln had visited personally. One was Gettysburg, Pennsylvania, and the other Dixon.

However, at that time, no marker, tablet or sign designated the Dixon location. In fact, not many outside the community itself actually knew that Lincoln had served part of his only federal military service in the 1832 Black Hawk War at Fort Dixon.

In the period from 1916 to 1930, many proposals were made and legislative measures undertaken to secure a permanent memorial to the nation's Civil War leader. However, it was not until the centennial celebration of Dixon's founding that the now-famous statue of Lincoln as a young militiaman was finally unveiled.

Dixon's first airport was established in 1925 when Henry Burdick and Frank McClanahan rented 50 acres of farm land for $100 per year across Illinois Route 38 from the present Walgreen Field. The second air field was a grass strip area now known as Industrial Park east of Dixon. This property was made available to flyers by Charles R. Walgreen when he offered to pay the $5 per acre annual rent for 160 acres of land then owned by Abner Barlow. A small hanger and office building were constructed on this field that was dedicated in 1930 as part of the activities of the Dixon Centennial Celebration. The photograph shows the large crowd gathered in September, 1930 to watch the airshow and dedication ceremonies for the city's new airport.

In 1933, a federal Civil Works Administration (CWA) project was approved to construct a new hanger for Dixon's third airport. Dement Schuler, chairman of the Dixon Airport Board, purchased 150 acres of land, which the present airport now occupies, for $17,400. Schuler carried the fund balance until paid in full by the city years later. Using 10,000 feet of streetcar track from the defunct Sterling, Dixon and Eastern Railway together with paving bricks from Dixon city streets, a large hanger was constructed on the field. The present airport was dedicated October 28, 1934 by Illinois Governor Henry Horner and Dement Schuler's World War I flying companion, Major Jimmy Doolittle. The original grass runway airport can be seen across the highway from the present Dixon Municipal Airport in this 1951 photograph.

The Airport Grill at the entrance of the local airport was a popular gathering place for over 30 years. A nearby gas station serviced local cars for many years.

A large crowd gathered on July 12, 1964, when the local airport was renamed the Charles R. Walgreen Field. Concrete runways were constructed in 1953 (2,800 feet in length) and in 1960 (3,100 feet long). Additional hangers and facilities were also added. The original hanger is named to honor Reinhardt Schnell, a local early-day aviation pioneer.

The architect's rendering of the proposed Dixon National Bank was first published early in 1912. Close examination of the drawing will show how closely the finished building, opened in 1914, looked like the proposed structure.

WILLIAM J. McALPINE

Contractor and architect William J. McAlpine was responsible for many of Dixon's finest and largest building projects. Born in Ashtabula, Ohio in 1852, McAlpine came to Illinois in 1887 to work as an architect in DeKalb. He was given his first commission in Dixon to build the O.B. Dodge home on West Third Street and became a resident of the community in 1888. One of the most successful and prominent contractors in the area, he was responsible for building the Lee County Courthouse in 1900-01, the Dixon Opera House in 1903, the Dixon Post Office in 1909, the Dixon National Bank in 1914, the Dixon Theatre and additions to the Reynolds Wire factory in 1922, the City National Bank in 1926 and the office building of the Illinois Northern Utilities Company. McAlpine also constructed courthouses in various cities in Illinois, Iowa and Wisconsin as well as the Geneva State Training School for Girls and the first buildings of the State Normal School in DeKalb. McAlpine constructed his home at the corner of East 2nd Street and South Ottawa Avenue where the Jones Funeral Home is now located. The well known builder died in Dixon on March 30, 1930, at the age of 78.

The Dixon National Bank is shown here under construction in 1912. Contractor for the tallest building in Dixon was William J. McAlpine who built many of the community's largest buildings.

POST OFFICE

Dixon's first post office was located in the log cabin home of "Father" John Dixon, often times in his hat band. Various rented locations also served as facilities through the years. As Dixon grew, it was finally deemed advisable for the federal government to obtain land on which to later construct a large federal building. The site selected was at the corner of West Second Street and South Galena Avenue across the avenue from the Lee County Courthouse and directly next to the Nachusa House. It became known as "Government Park" with construction on the proposed $60,000 postal facility started in August, 1909. Ground was broken then with B.F. Shaw, postmaster, then in his 19th year of federal service, acting as coordinator of the event.

Ironically, Shaw did not live to see the new edifice completed as he died a short month later on September 18, 1909. Finally, on March 11, 1911, thousands of local citizens attended the opening day events of the newly opened federal mail facility that then had 20 employees. All agreed the $90,000 (the building ran $30,000 over anticipated costs), 5,000 square-foot post office was "top rate." Made of Bedford stone, marble, granite, steel and terrazzo, its front door alone cost $8,000. The post office served the community well for 51 years until the 9,462 square-foot leased facility at the corner of Highland Avenue and West Second Street was dedicated on February 14, 1963.

From the time of its opening in 1911, the Dixon Post Office has been the subject of countless post card views such as this early issue.

In 1936, Postmaster John Moyer, sixth from the left in the front row, and his able crew of postal employees posed in front of the Dixon Post Office.

Edward Vaile and George O'Malley owned and operated a men's clothing store at 110 West First Street in downtown Dixon for many years. This photograph shows, left to right, Clark Rickert, Al Buckaloo, H. Stephens, George O'Malley, Edward Vaile, Aggie Schumard and Edward Bennett posing in front of the popular clothing store.

VAILE AND O'MALLEY CLOTHING STORE

Vaile and O'Malley moved their men's furnishings store to 122 West First Street before 1910. This interior view of the store shows the large stock of men's clothing the two merchants carried.

A more up-to-date interior view of the Vaile and O'Malley Clothing Store can be seen in this photograph. Customer Ken Mall can be seen with store personnel Robert Bovey, Edward Vaile and Royal Fitzsimmons in the early 1950's.

Vaile Clothiers succeeded the original store and remained an excellent outlet for men's clothing through the years until the early 1960's when the store closed.

LAING FEED MILL

The George D. Laing Feed Mill was one of the most widely known feed mills in northwest Illinois. The firm was established in a small frame building located on West River Street facing the Rock River in 1872. Robert F. Laing, contractor in 1851 of the Illinois Central Railroad bridge and street arches, started the business. After his death on December 4, 1873, the feed mill was operated by his son, George D. Laing.

In 1890, John T. Laing joined his brother in the feed and grain operation and together they built the imposing three-story brick feed mill and elevator pictured. A later elevator and mill were added to the extensive feed grinding operation.

The business was continued after the death of George D. Laing in 1915 and following the demise of John Thomas Laing in 1936, the firm was sold. Willard E. Beanblossom purchased the business enterprise in the fall of 1936 after moving to Dixon from Iowa.

Following the death of Beanblossom, the feed mill and elevator property was leased and later purchased by the City of Dixon for use as a parking lot.

Mrs. J.O. Trippeer, wife of the owner of the Rock River Poultry Company, is shown here feeding the prize winning chickens she and her husband raised. A display of ribbons and awards, won by the couple at the St. Louis Fair, can be seen to Mrs. Trippeer's left.

ROCK RIVER POULTRY COMPANY

The Rock River has provided countless hours of enjoyment, contemplation and pleasurable pastimes from the very first days of Dixon. At first considered a navigable stream by early settlers, it was soon determined that the river would furnish Dixonites with recreation rather than commerce. Typical of the small steam driven boats to ply the Rock River was the *White Swan* pictured here with its unusual display of flags.

Boating on the Rock River near Myers Island upstream from Dixon was a popular endeavor of Dixonites. For several years, a regular routine of passenger carrying boats traveled between Grand Detour and Dixon with tourists and local citizens.

The steamboat *City of Dixon* was a common sight on the Rock River for many years. The boat, with its moveable paddlewheel, traveled from Assembly Park to Lowell Park and downstream to a point north of the Rock River dam for many years. The vessel was owned and operated by Robert H. Espy, Boatman, who resided at 416 E. Third Street.

The Howell launch *Emma* carried passengers up and down the Rock River from Assembly Park to Lowell Park on a regular basis each summer. The steam-driven launch could carry up to two dozen passengers.

The banks of the Rock River were popular picnic places for those who enjoyed the beauty of the river. This group, on a Sunday row boat ride on the river, took time out from their fun to have their pictures taken by a family photographer.

A clammer's camp can be seen from the Rock River. The favorite pastime of many from the late 1800's onward, clamming on the Rock River gave others a profitable source of income. The clam shells were ground and used for several purposes including feed for chickens and use in the manufacture of inexpensive buttons. "Pearls" removed were also sold to brokers for use in various manufacturing endeavors.

This clammer's camp included a tent for overnight stays, a flat boat with clam nets in place and the usual pile of opened clam shells from which "pearls" and food had been removed.

This large collection of Rock River clam shells shows a method of storage. By keeping them in this condition until they were completely dry, they could be sold to brokers. Clamming on the Rock River gave Dixonites an almost unending supply of clams for over 50 years.

From 1904 on, the annual Labor Day Dixon Elks Club "Clambake" was an important event in the community. Originally held on an island in the Rock River with excursion boats carrying passengers to the site, thousands attended from all over Illinois, Iowa and Wisconsin. Locations were changed often and in 1940, the event was held in the clubrooms of the sponsoring organization. At first, profits were in the $1-2,000 range annually but they dwindled until toward the end of the clambake era in Dixon only 35¢ was realized at the final event held.

Orville Westgor's Orchestra was a permanent fixture at the Dixon Theatre from 1924 until the advent of sound motion pictures ended the days of vaudeville and live music on the theatre's stage. This 1924 photograph was taken in front of a popular Dixon Theatre backdrop and includes, left to right, Sam Samuelson, Caroline Westgor, Orville Westgor, Flora Horner, James Jarvis, Mr. Kellman and Edwin Arthus. Westgor, creator of the theme song for Dixon's annual Petunia Festival, has been involved in the Dixon music scene for over 65 years as school music instructor, band leader and music store owner.

The Alaskans, pictured here in their "Igloo" created on the stage of the Masonic Temple in the early 1930's, was led by Clifford Floto. Known locally as "The Hot Band With The Cold Name," members of the band, from left to right, are: back row, Alex Groehling, Harry Hintz, Curtis Rice; front row, Myrtle Bishop, Emil Manifici, Orchestra Leader Floto, Clinton "Pete" Ives, Ken Ketchin, Harold Spencer and John V. Hoon.

Walter C. Knack, when employed by the American Tobacco Company to teach farmers how to roll fifty cigarettes from a pouch of tobacco, drove this open car in 1916. Knack began business in Dixon in 1923 at 305 West First Street as a wholesale tobacco distributor. In an era when hard roads were the exception, he promised his customers delivery of their orders within 24-hours. Some of these accounts were 20-30 miles away and presented an on-going challenge to the growing wholesale concern.

In the middle 1930's, the W.C. Knack Company sent these six automobiles throughout Northern Illinois to solicit business for the firm. The six company salesmen and their employer are pictured left to right: Lawrence Grove, Frank Gardner, Clarence Meyers, Carroll Yeast, Walter C. Knack, Charles Kock and David Kirk.

DIXON DAIRIES

The Coss Dairy, from 1917 to 1936, delivered their milk and dairy products from horse-driven carts such as this model.

Henry W. Hey was a familiar figure around Dixon for many years delivering milk and dairy products from a vehicle such as this Hill Den Farm Dairy Products truck.

In 1936, Coss Dairy switched their delivery vehicles to motorized cars and trucks. Shown here, in 1937, is part of the Coss Dairy fleet of vehicles and their owners and salesmen.

A complete listing of all the various Dixon dairies down through the passing years would fill volumes. From the 1860's when Mr. Mason delivered his milk to housewives, the community has had many outstanding milk producing facilities.

The George Page Anglo-Swiss Condensed Milk Company was a leader in the local dairy industry. The Borden Company and Dean Foods, Inc. enterprises following the Page business have contributed greatly to the local dairy industry.

Among others, the McAlister Dairy (which operated out of the basement of the Dixon Hotel), the Max Logan Dairy on Jefferson Avenue and East Bradshaw Street and Othendahl's Dairy on Brinton Avenue all contributed to Dixon's milk supply at one time or another. Likewise, names such as Steinbaugh, Turner, Fulfs, Belcher, Senneff and Drew are all connected to the history of the Dixon milk business.

In 1917, Oscar Coss started the Fernwood Farm Dairy. In 1921, his sons, Leslie and Harold ("Barney") built a plant at 112 E. Everett Street and 15 years later, in 1936, retired their last horse driven milk wagon in favor of motor transportation.

The Standard Dairy began in 1935 with Earl Auman in charge for Union Dairy Company. This plant later became the Amboy Condensed Milk plant under the direction of Verne Johnson. The business was later operated by Mason Hopkins as the Fairview Farm Dairy and still later by Otto Weber and his sons, William and Norbert.

1937 saw the addition of the Lawton Farm in Palmyra Township to the list of local dairies. In 1941, the first downtown dairy store run by the Lawtons was opened at 315 West First Street and in 1947, the first of several dairy bars was begun. A large plant complex on West 7th Street was operated for many years by the firm.

Earl Prince operated a successful retail ice cream shop business from a location on East River Street. Prince Ice Cream Castles were located throughout Northern Illinois for decades with all the company's production centering in Dixon.

The Hill Den Farm Dairy Products Company, operated by Henry W. Hey, was a prime supplier of milk to area residents for years. The firm's slogan, "You Can Whip Our Cream But You Can't Beat Our Milk", can still be recalled by Dixonites.

The Fairview Dairy building, located on South Galena Avenue, was a long time Dixon landmark.

Lawton's Dairy conducted their extensive wholesale-retail dairy business from this multi-building complex for many years. Located on West 7th Street, the Lawton operation employed over 100 employees at one time.

The Dixon Ice and Fuel Company and Prince Ice Cream Castles operation was located on East River Street at Artesian Avenue. Vehicles delivered products throughout Northern Illinois that were made in this building complex.

THE FLOOD OF 1937

In March, 1937, one of the community's worst floods caused damage then estimated to be in the millions of dollars. The entire Dixon High School was surrounded with water from the Rock River that had rolled over its banks. School was dismissed for several days until the raging water subsided.

Dixon's National Guard Armory was dedicated October 5, 1939, on the same day officials of the State of Illinois dedicated the Abraham Lincoln Memorial Bridge over the Rock River at Galena Avenue. The National Guard Armory, constructed with state and federal Works Project Administration (WPA) funds, cost $225,148 while the bridge, built by the State of Illinois, cost $316,500 to construct 48 years ago.

NATIONAL GUARD ARMORY

Lincoln School on South Lincoln Avenue at West Fifth Street, opened January 23, 1938, with Miss Esther Barton as Principal. Constructed at a cost of $273,000, the new grade school replaced the 1866 E.C. Smith School on West 7th Street, Truman School on West Third Street and Woodworth School that had been built to serve Dementtown area children. A statue of Abraham Lincoln as a seven-year-old boy given as a gift to the school by Mrs. Ruth Walgreen Franklin, daughter of Mr. and Mrs. Charles R. Walgreen, was presented to Lincoln School on October 10, 1947.

This dual control student driving automobile appeared in front of the Dixon High School in 1941. The car is shown here being examined by Illinois State Patrolman George Ives, High School Principal B.J. Frazer and his Assistant as well as the driver training class of the school.

GEORGE C. LOVELAND, CIRCA 1866

GEORGE C. LOVELAND, CIRCA 1925

The Loveland Community House, 513 West Second Street, was a gift to Dixon area citizens given by Mr. and Mrs. George C. Loveland. The Loveland family had settled in Dixon in 1837 and had been active in the real estate and insurance business in Dixon. George and Emma Loveland had no children and no one to whom to leave their inheritance. When Loveland died in 1928, his will saw to it his wife was adequately provided for. Following her death in 1938, a committee was formed to select a site on the south side of the Rock River to construct a community house. Loveland's will also stipulated a part of the building be used to house a museum. Dedicated on October 8, 1940, the Loveland Community House was built by the George Lindquist Construction Company at a cost of approximately $200,000. The generosity of Mr. and Mrs. George C. Loveland to the Dixon community has given local citizens the use of an outstanding building for the past 47 years.

LOVELAND COMMUNITY HOUSE

The old Read and Burright Livery Stable served as the home of Hey Brothers Ice Cream from 1922 to 1946. Construction of a new building took almost two years due to wartime shortages.

The stick novelty production room, utilized until recent years to produce fudge bars, ice cream bars, etc. and other frozen confections, contained up-to-date equipment during its years of use. Hey Brothers employees shown, in 1962, are left to right, N.H. Madden, Carlton Routh, Emil Hey and Ruth Kump.

A partnership of four Hey brothers began in the dairy business in Sterling in 1906. One of the brothers, Henry M. Hey, moved to Dixon in 1919 to purchase Ben Snyder's Dixon Ice Cream Company, 314 West First Street. In 1922, the ice cream company, then called Hey Brothers Ice Cream, purchased the former stable building at the corner of West First Street and Madison Avenue.

Henry Hey and his two sons, Dean and James, and his daughter, Beulah, formed a partnership in 1941 and began construction of a new brick manufacturing plant at 424 West First Street in 1946. An open house tour of the new facility was held on Memorial Day, 1948.

The family-owned wholesale ice cream business is today one of the few independent operations of its kind in Illinois. The firm distributes their product throughout northern Illinois, southeast Wisconsin and eastern Iowa.

WAR MEMORIAL ARCH

The Dixon War Memorial Arch on South Galena Avenue was built at a cost of approximately $465 by contractor W.D. Baum in 1910. It was intended to be only a temporary structure to be disassembled after a welcome home parade for veterans of World War I. Shortly after the ceremonies, a Victory Memorial Arch Committee was formed to insure a permanent structure would be built and maintained.

An addition to the Galena Avenue Arch was a flagpole at the top and hanging globes with letters spelling out the word WELCOME.

The wording on the War Memorial Arch was maintained for several years until painted out and substituted with the words "DIXON" on either side. This Arch, made mostly of wood, stood through the years with spasmodic repaintings of its outer shell until 1944.

The Arch was taken down in November, 1944, and replaced with a permanent concrete and steel version at a cost of approximately $8,000. Funds for the memorial to men of World War I and World War II who gave their lives for their country, was contributed by citizens of Dixon and Lee County.

This version of the War Memorial Arch lasted 16 years until 1965 when the reconstruction and widening of Galena Avenue through Dixon forced its retirement from the local scene.

The annual holiday season saw the addition of Santa Claus and his reindeer, done in bright neon, flying over the War Memorial Arch. This was a welcome sight for children and drew crowds each Christmas season.

157

Dixon's War Memorial Arch was replaced across a four-lane Galena Avenue in January, 1966. The redesigned and freshly painted Arch featured a wider span. It was dedicated on Memorial Day, 1966.

Suffering the aches and pains of 20 years of use, the War Memorial Arch was taken down in 1985. This Arch, at different times, carried a symbol of the "Petunia City", and later, a sign noting Dixon to be the home of Ronald Reagan. Dedicated on Veteran's Day, 1985, the new fiberglass War Memorial Arch is expected to last several decades.

WORLD WAR II ON THE HOME FRONT

In June, 1943, Dixon Mayor William V. Slothower hammers away at the community scrap pile located on Hennepin Avenue. The Mayor, in the center of the photograph, has the help of Albert Fordyce and Jack Plotkin.

In March, 1945, Dixon Cub and Boy Scouts gathered 35,600 pounds of wastepaper to contribute to the war effort. Pictured here, standing, are Eugene Hollbrook, Jack K. Klavohn, Phil Kerz and Steve Christ. Kneeling are Ronald Anders, James Schertner, Wayne Thomas and Norman Stripe.

During the war years of World War II, those on the home front assisted in the war effort by tending Victory Gardens. These young men are shown planting a large garden area to grow scarce food items.

V-J Day, the end of World War II, saw the end of gas rationing. And no one in Dixon seemed happier than gasoline station operator Pete O'Malley or customer W.R. Keeley.

This Serviceman's Booth was located at the Dixon Ration Board. It was erected by the Lee County War Dads and operated by the Service Mother's Club. Pictured here during World War II are, left to right, PFC Dwain J. Baux, Mrs. I.B. Hoefer, Lt. John P. Abbott and Lt. Joseph A. Garland.

As part of a War Bond Drive in Dixon on September 20, 1943, this aerial bomb was autographed by, left to right, Earl Kennedy, F.A. Hansen and E.S. Wadsworth.

MEMORIAL POOL

On June 27, 1950, voters of the Dixon Park District passed a $120,000 bond issue to construct the Dixon Memorial Pool. These funds, together with a $30,000 grant from the Loveland Community House Trust Fund, saw the construction of an above-ground 30,000 gallon swimming facility. An Injun Summer Days celebration, attended by Ronald "Dutch" Reagan in 1950, saw the hometown motion picture star dedicate the community's new swimming pool. After long years of service, the pool was closed and later remodeled before being reopened again in the summer of 1985.

LOUELLA PARSONS

Louella Parsons was born in Freeport, Illinois and moved to Dixon as a small child. She attended Dixon High School and Dixon Business College and after graduation was employed by the *Dixon Sun* newspaper as society editor, drama and music critic and general reporter. The young newspaper reporter married Jack Parsons and moved to Burlington, Iowa, later moving to California.

Louella Parsons wrote the world's first motion picture newspaper column in 1913, making her name a household word wherever movies were seen or discussed. In 1925, she went to work for William Randolph Hearst at the *Chicago Herald* and three years later, conducted her first radio interview program.

Parsons was the author of two books, contributor to the Encyclopedia Britannica and star in several movies including *Hollywood Hotel* in 1934. Parsons' radio show was heard over 250 stations and her daily newspaper column was read by 40,000,000 readers in the United States and abroad.

In 1941, "Louella Parsons Day" was held in Dixon in her honor with all proceeds from the homecoming celebration benefiting the KSB Public Hospital. In addition to Parsons, Ronald "Dutch" Reagan, Bob Hope, Jerry Colona, Bebe Daniels, Ben Lyons and several other Hollywood celebrities attended the local celebration.

Motion picture star Ronald "Dutch" Reagan rode in the Injun Summer Days Parade in August, 1950, much to the delight of all his fans and old friends.

RONALD REAGAN

A notice of prime local importance was spread across the front page of the *Dixon Evening Telegraph* on September 27, 1937. The feature dealt with the announcement that Ronald "Dutch" Reagan's first motion picture *Love Is On The Air* would be shown at the Lee Theatre. The movie premiere was scheduled as part of Dixon's annual Fall Festival and Corn Show.

From this time on Dixon's own movie star became a legend in his chosen field of entertainment. His visit to Dixon as part of Louella Parson's Day in September, 1941, is well remembered by Dixonites. Reagan and Parsons were accompanied to Dixon by Bob Hope, Jerry Colona, Ben Lyons and Bebe Daniels, Ann Rutherford, George Montgomery and other Hollywood stars.

Nine years later "Dutch" Reagan once again returned to his hometown to participate in the Injun Summer Days celebration of August, 1950.

Surrounded by local lovelies, "Dutch" Reagan was photographed for a family album collection just before the start of the 1950 parade.

Riding a beautiful horse, "Dutch" Reagan waved to the crowds that lined a long parade route through downtown Dixon during the 1950 Dixon Injun Summer Days celebration.

CENTENNIAL EDITION

The *Dixon Evening Telegraph* celebrated the 100th anniversary of their newspaper publication career on May 1, 1951. At this time, a 272 page Centennial Edition was printed containing 16 sections of chronological history of the Dixon area. It took 13,818 man hours to produce the paper and a multiplicity of people to distribute this massive edition.

The press crew of the *Dixon Evening Telegraph* check the cover page of the Centennial Edition as it came off the press. The men are, left to right, Leo Chandler, Don Mercer, Lester Spencer, Clarence Harshbarger, Ab Haistenberg, LeRoy Dodd and Carl Blades.

Dixon High School students look down a long line of stacks of Centennial Edition newspapers in the Dixon Armory. The stacks of newspapers ran the full length of the building on both sides of the main floor. The pictured students are, left to right, Benny Roe, Wayne Ackerman, Douglas Wadsworth, and Ronnie LaFever.

A small army of circulation workers put together the 16-section special Centennial Edition of the *Dixon Evening Telegraph* in May, 1951. The paper went to 13,000 homes in a three county area plus hundreds of mailed issues that were sent across the nation.

MABEL S. SHAW

Mabel S. Shaw, born in Darlington, Wisconsin on September 17, 1870, was publisher of the *Dixon Evening Telegraph* for 46 years. As a teenager, she came to Dixon to attend classes at the Dixon Business College where she met the eldest son of B.F. Shaw, Eustace E. Shaw. She married Eustace, who was associated with his father in the publication of the *Dixon Evening Telegraph,* in 1889 when she was 19 years old.

Eustace and Mabel Shaw had three sons: George, Benjamin and Robert. In 1902 at the early age of 45, Eustace Shaw died leaving his widow to raise their family. When B.F. Shaw died seven years later in 1909, Mabel Shaw assumed control of the B.F. Shaw Printing Company which included the local newspaper.

For the next 46 years, Mrs. Shaw successfully operated the publishing company in addition to managing her far-flung financial and industrial interests which included being a representative on the boards of many corporations and financial institutions.

When the *Dixon Evening Telegraph* celebrated its centennial in 1951, Editor George Shaw wrote of his mother:
> "One of her strongest convictions was the belief that no business could afford to stand still. It must constantly improve, expand and progress, she maintained."

Mabel Shaw personally directed the restoration and remodeling of the historic Nachusa House in the mid-1950's. She did not, regretfully, live to see the old hotel re-open. After a long, busy, life, Mrs. Shaw died on March 7, 1955 at the age of 84.

SHERWOOD DIXON

Illinois Lieutenant Governor Sherwood Dixon and Democratic candidate for President of the United States Adlai Stevenson II are shown in an informal pose during their 1952 political campaigns.

Sherwood Dixon, a direct descendant of "Father" John Dixon, was born June 19, 1896 in Dixon. He attended North Dixon High School and was a 1920 graduate of the University of Notre Dame where he played and coached football under Knute Rockne. Dixon married Helen M. Cahill in 1933. An Army veteran of World War I and of the National Guard in World War II, Dixon also served on the General Staff of the War Department. He retired with the rank of Brigadier General from the Illinois National Guard in 1951. Dixon was a member and president of the Dixon School Board, chairman of the Lee County Democratic Committee and served as United States Referee in Bankruptcy for the Western Division, Northern District of Illinois from 1954 to 1971. Sherwood Dixon was elected Lieutenant Governor of Illinois under Governor Adlai Stevenson II in 1949 and was drafted by his party in 1952 to run for the office of Governor of Illinois when Governor Stevenson was nominated for the office of President of the United States. Dixon waged a long but unsuccessful campaign for the governorship but was later defeated by Republican William G. Stratton. Governor Dixon resided at his home in Dixon until his death at the age of 76 on May 17, 1973.

SCHOOL PRINCIPALS

In 1954, the four principals of Dixon's grade schools met to have this informal photograph taken. This foursome of dedicated educators each served the local school system for many years. From left to right, they are: Mary Buchanan, South Central School; Molly Duffy, Washington School; Esther Barton, Lincoln School; and Edith Scholl, Jefferson School.

LOVELAND SCHOOL

George C. Loveland, in 1913, gave a site valued at the time at $1,500, in addition to $6,000 in cash, toward the construction of this three-story brick grade school building. The Loveland School, in northwest Dixon, was approved by voters of North Dixon on June 23, 1913 by a vote of 174-3. Pictured here in 1951, the grade school served for many years as a neighborhood grade school and local area social center.

The Hintz Studio was a very evident part of the Dixon scene for many years. This photograph of the interior of the Hintz Photo Studio, 111 East First Street, was taken in 1910 for publication in the *Dixon Evening Telegraph's* "Prospectus of Dixon." Many of the Hintz pictures taken from the turn-of-the-century through the 1950's record the passing of time in Dixon and are considered prime examples of the art of photography.

The Hintz Studio changed with the times as can be noted in this mid-1950's photograph. Barbara (Shippert) Weidman, left, and Olive Klingman were both devoted employees of the photography business.

ONE WAY STREETS

A noble experiment that was doomed to failure was a limited one way street system in downtown Dixon. This photograph, taken October 7, 1955, at the corner of West Second Street and Hennepin Avenue, shows local businessman Paul Potts and Chief of Police Earl Kelchner watching Frank McIntyre, city traffic maintenance worker, removing covers placed over a one-way traffic sign.

The one way street program included First Street west bound and Second Street east bound between Madison Avenue and Galena Avenue. The street plan was given a 90-day trail and at the end of that time span the majority of merchants in downtown Dixon opposed the idea so it was abandoned.

One of Dixon's favorite hang-outs was Tony's, a downtown soda fountain business on South Galena Avenue. Pictured here behind the counter, between two of his professional soda jerks, is owner-operator Tony Bevilacqua. Here you could drink fresh coffee or have a sparkling coke for 5¢, a soda for 15¢ and a thick, heavy, malted milk or shake for 20¢. Loungers were welcome to meet and discuss the events of the day at Tony's, one of Dixon's landmarks for many years.

TONY'S

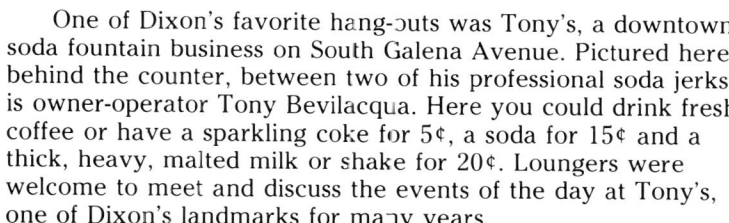

ALMOND E. MORRISON

Born and raised in southern Illinois, Almond Morrison moved to Dixon in 1942. Morrison was connected with the sport of baseball for over 34 years, 18 of which he was an active player. Among other teams, he played with the Sparta Stars, Sparta, Illinois and the GROP Freeman of Dixon. Following his years as a baseball player, Al Morrison organized the Lee County Umpires Association of which he became president. He umpired in the Dixon Jaycee League, the Dixon Merchants League and the Dixon Church Softball League over the years. In 1965, he was presented a plaque by the Dixon Jaycee organization in appreciation for his long years of service to the youth of Dixon. Following his death in 1968, the Al Morrison Baseball League was named in his honor.

EURITH LEYDIG

One of the kindest, most compassionate, women ever to reside in Dixon, Eurith Leydig was born November 8, 1886. Mrs. Leydig devoted 55 years of her life to the betterment of the poor and needy of Dixon and surrounding areas. She filled her home with donated and acquired clothing, toys and other articles to share with others. Over the years countless thousands of items passed through the kindly hands of Eurith Leydig into the hands of those truly in need. Mrs. Leydig was a long-time music teacher and served as church organist for the First United Methodist Church for many years. She was a member of the KSB Hospital board of directors for 33 years and a charter member of the Dixon Dance Club. During the Depression of the 1930's, Mrs. Leydig assisted local doctors in the home delivery of babies as well as spending countless hours easing the trying times for those suffering the effects of the Depression. The Eurith Leydig Memorial Center at West Sixth Street and Highland Avenue continues today to serve those in need. When Eurith Leydig died in June, 1970, she left a legacy of care and concern for her fellow human beings rarely equalled anywhere.

These ten young men were Dixon's 1967 Bronco League Champs. Coached by Charles "Pete" Webster and George Oswalt, the Hey Brothers baseball team well represents all the hundreds of young boys and girls in the community who have participated over the years in the large summer baseball program. The baseball players are: front row: Greg Mullery and Mike Mercer; second row: Scott Smith, Thomas Ruffin, Mark Youngren and Tom Wakely; third row: Robert Le Blanc, Chuck Webster, Gary Oswalt and Cleve Burkitt; back row: Coach Charles "Pete" Webster and Manager George Oswalt.

CHAPTER V

MODERN YEARS

1960 - Present

The first year of the Sixties in Dixon was a "bad news - good news" period. The Dixon City Council, in 1961, heard reports that in excess of 7,000 elm trees were dead or dying and had to be removed; while the local industrial committee purchased 150 acres of land for an Industrial Park east along Route 38 in February of the same year. The bad news of dead trees and the good news of industrial activity served to remind Dixonites that an era of change was about to begin.

In the year that John F. Kennedy defeated Richard M. Nixon for the Presidency of the United States, Dixonites saw their downtown A & P Grocery move to West Third Street and Madison Avenue while Conley's Market opened at West First Street and South Peoria Avenue. Shinner's Meat Market was replaced by Fulmer's Card Shop and Ames Furniture expanded into the former *Dixon Evening Telegraph* building on East First Street. The City National Bank enlarged and replaced Cook's Flowers, Cobb Optical, Maloney Cleaners and Dixon Camera Center along East First Street; at the same time, First Federal Savings and Loan Association opened for business at 119 South Galena Avenue.

A mixed bag of industrial activity gave Dixonites something to talk about in 1961. In the winter months, Freeman Shoe Company laid off 100 workers with the company later being purchased by the H.O. Toor Shoe Company. C.J. Glasgow purchased the former Green River Ordnance Plant property and the Borden Company ended their evaporated and condensed milk operation in Dixon. The best news of the year was the announcement that Shurhit Manufacturing Company was to open a new plant in Dixon and the Dixon State School was to increase by 212 their employee work force.

In September of that year, National Standard Wire Company informed their 350 employees that a 69¢ per hour wage cut was necessary or they would see the former Reynolds Wire operation close. This depressing news was magnified by a $100,000 fire that destroyed the J.J. Newberry Variety Store and F.W. Woolworth business on West First Street. Another equally bad fire burned the Club Cafe and Barriage Appliance Company on East First Street.

When the Cuban missile crisis reached its height and John Glenn became the first American to orbit the earth, a $200,000 property damage fire struck the Dixon Mills in Dementtown. Another large fire heavily damaged the United Lunch and Tap, Hank Henry's Clothing Store and three other business places on South Galena Avenue in the winter of 1962.

The Beier Bread Company, a local firm since 1869, closed with 375 people put out of work early in 1962. National Standard Wire Company also permanently closed their Dixon operation in March. The following month it was announced that Daubert Chemical Company of Chicago would locate in a $40,000 building in Dixon's Industrial Park and Beier and Company, a Chicago based paper products firm, would locate in the former East End Plant of the old Reynolds Wire Company. At the same time, the C.K. Willett Consulting firm took over the former office building on East Third Street that had formerly housed the local headquarters of the Reynolds Wire firm.

The following year, 1963, 14 acres of land in Dixon's Industrial Park was purchased by General Cable Company for the construction of a million dollar building that would house 200 employees. In April of that year, Raynor Manufacturing Company began a 12,000 foot addition to their large overhead door manufacturing business on East River Road.

The first Dixon Petunia Festival was held over the July 4th weekend of 1964; an event that would find a permanent place in the future scheme of things in Dixon. A $220,000 fire destroyed the West First Street plant of Blackhawk Photo Mount Company with the result that the company moved into new quarters in the former Beier Bread building on East River Street and Ottawa Avenue.

1964 saw the beginnings of the national "War on Poverty" when Lyndon B. Johnson defeated Barry Goldwater for President of the United States. The year also saw the Allied Chain Company move into new quarters at the Green River Ordnance Plant. A disastrous downtown $200,000 fire destroyed the Eckman V & S Hardware store on West First Street with the result that the Cahill Electric Company later moved into the space.

The Admiral Corporation radio division, in 1964, leased the old East River Street Reynolds Wire building and within four days had a 30 worker assembly line in operation. The corporation later purchased a five-acre site in Dixon's Industrial Park on which to build a 150,000 square-foot factory at a cost of over $1,000,000.

1965 was the first year of classes at Sauk Valley College near Dixon with Dr. Edward J. Sabol serving as the college's first president. The same year, a YMCA fund drive began with the intention of raising $545,645 to build a new facility for the rejuvenated organization; a funding effort that was to eventually raise far in excess of its original goal.

The nation had over 400,000 troops in Viet Nam in 1966, the year downtown streets in Dixon were torn out to be replaced with new and modern thoroughfares. The Dixon Home Telephone Company remodeled and expanded and the Dixon State School's 164-bed medical and surgical facility was built in the same year.

The term "hippie" became a part of the language in 1967. This was the year, too, that the Admiral Corporation employed 2,500 workers in Dixon, that Sauk Valley Cleaners began a long history of retail business and a $200,000 bond issue was passed locally for an expansion of the Dixon Public Library.

The Borden Company closed their Dixon facility completely in 1968 while in the next year work began on the extension of the East-West Tollway that would pass just south of Dixon.

The Rogers Printing Company, begun in 1908 as Rogers and Owen, was purchased in 1922 by O.M. Rogers. It first operated in the 100 block of East First Street and moved in 1927 to 307 West First Street. The book publishers went out of business early in 1969 and their building later gave way to a city parking lot.

Anchor Coupling Company came to Dixon in 1969, the same year Admiral Corporation left Dixon with a large empty industrial building. Harney's TV and Farley's Appliance opened that year at 83 South Peoria Avenue and in the fall, Payless Foods Store began local operations.

The following year "Earth Day" was observed in April. Three longtime downtown retail stores closed in 1970; Ford Hopkins Drug Store, Walgreen Drug Store and Vaile's Clothing Store. In the same year, the *Dixon Evening Telegraph* changed from a letterpress operation to offset printing of its daily newspaper and Aqua Aquariums-Pampered Pets opened for business.

Annual inflation was at 5% in 1971 while a 6% unemployment figure was noted in Dixon. Barry Royster and Kay Draper moved their barber shop business when the building at 224 West First Street was demolished. The structure, built in 1903, had housed barber Harry Stephans until 1944 and then, E.M. "Cotton" Green until 1970.

A highlight of 1971 was the September Centennial Celebration of the founding of the Dixon National Bank. Celebrated in high style, the community would long remember the interesting events of the bank's week-long birthday.

Flex-O-Glass purchased the General Cable plant in Dixon's Industrial Park in 1971 and the Viking Sewing Shop opened for business in downtown Dixon. Also, the lease between the City of Dixon and Lee County for shared use of the new Law Enforcement Center established it as the first joint use facility of its kind in Illinois.

The year President Richard M. Nixon defeated Senator George McGovern for President, E.E. Edelmann and Company purchased and moved into the former Admiral Corporation building. 1972 found Hardware Wholesalers becoming the first occupants of the new Tollway Industrial Park south of Dixon.

Another industrial change took place when the Donaldson Company, in 1973, moved to Dixon. The following year, when President Nixon resigned and Vice President Gerald Ford became President, the extension of the East-West Tollway opened. The 69 million dollar project carried its first paying customers in November, 1974.

The Freeman Shoe Company plant, a Dixon landmark for almost 90 years, was demolished in 1975. In this same year, the Rock River bridge at Peoria Avenue was reconstructed at a cost of over $600,000. In the year of the national Bicentennial celebration, 1976, Dixon's Petunia Festival was the area's top-flight July 4th attraction. 1972 also saw the Dixon Publishing Company, a longtime industrial mainstay in the community, merged into the ownership of the Sleepeck Company, a Chicago based firm.

Lowell Park grew in size in 1977 by nearly 50 acres when the Dixon Park Board accepted the land donation of Charles R. Walgreen II "with gratitude." A new Dixon Rural Fire Station was opened at the same time a new city hall project was turned down in favor of a remodeling of the 1906 facility.

New Year's Eve of 1978 was celebrated for $10 per couple at the Nachusa House. Earlier in the year veteran Dixon Police Chief Earl Kelchner retired after over 30 years of service to the city. In the next year, the Dixon Fruit Company warehouse at East River Street and Ottawa Avenue was demolished after its roof caved in during the January "Blizzard of '79". The building had been used, over the years, as a barrel factory, ice house, beer distribution center and storage facility.

Dixon's Ronald "Dutch" Reagan won a landslide victory over President Jimmy Carter in the fall of 1980. Carrying Dixon handily, Reagan was quickly pronounced the winner by the Dixon Evening Telegraph, thus becoming the first newspaper in the nation to proclaim the victory. Dixon became accustomed to the spotlight of national fame during and after Reagan's victory; a fame that continues to this day.

A total of 51 rehabilitation projects were introduced by a consulting firm early in 1981. These city-wide improvements were suggested for the development of a new and better Dixon. The Economy Lift Truck Company at 1100 West First Street was destroyed by fire in 1981. Dixonites by the hundreds attended the Presidential Inauguration that year and 482 jobs were cut from the payroll of the Dixon Development Center. During this time span, longtime Dixon City Fire Department Chief Edmund Pierce retired after over 30 years of service to the city.

The following year, the 64-year-old Dixon Developmental Center was permanently closed, to be replaced by the Dixon Correctional Center, a minimum security prison. In 1983, three new retail stores opened in downtown Dixon: Baskets & More, S.S. Update and Fashions, Ltd.

By 1984, Dixonites were sure their hometown hero, President Ronald Reagan, would be reelected in the fall. They were correct in their forecast and recalled, the first family's visit to Dixon for the February 6, 1984 birthday of the President. At that time, his boyhood home at 816 South Hennepin Avenue was dedicated while President Reagan noted, "My heart is still here and always will be."

An old local landmark, the Chicago and Northwestern Railroad Depot, was demolished in January, 1985 and a new fiberglass arch over Galena Avenue was constructed to "last 100 years." A spring flood sent huge iceblocks down the rampaging Rock River to rest on the Dixon High School football field and tennis courts; another reminder that the force of the Rock River was ever a threat to the peace and quiet of Dixon.

During 1986 and into 1987, Dixon's progress on several fronts remained in a poised position waiting for the future to unfold. Plans are on the drawing boards that will swiftly carry the community into the next decade before the next century at top speed. These changes covering a broad spectrum, will greatly enhance our community's ability to successfully meet the challenges of the years to come.

TICKETED HORSE

Dixon Police Officer Frank Chapman, a long time city policeman and parking meter maintenance man, was a man devoted to his duty. Here he can be seen in the early 1960's giving an overtime parking ticket to a horse tied up to one of the city's street meters. Whether the horse or its owner paid the overtime parking fee, Police Officer "Chappie" had done his duty.

GALENA AVENUE

Before 1960, the tree lined streets of Dixon were a thing of beauty. Branches intertwined over the streets making a tunnel-like avenue of green beauty all summer long. This view, looking south on North Galena Avenue, was typical of Dixon street scenes over a quarter of a century ago.

The removal of over 7,000 diseased trees from the streets and avenues of Dixon together with street improvement projects throughout the 1960's, gave Dixon a cold and barren look. This view, looking north on North Galena Avenue, was taken during the summer of 1962.

The love of beauty and pride in the appearance of their community led members of the Dixon Men's Garden Club to plant over 20,000 lovely petunia plants each year along over 3 miles of Dixon's main streets. In the 25 years that have passed since the first streets were lined with flowers, Dixon has received world-wide acclaim for its beautiful petunia edged thoroughfares. Dixon, " The Petunia City", will forever be in debt to the local Men's Garden Club for their efforts at beautifying their hometown.

FIRST AND GALENA

This photograph, circa 1920, was taken from the roof of the Dixon National Bank. It shows the Dixon Opera House on the left and the 1896 building located at the corner of South Galena Avenue and West First Street. The dome of the Lee County Courthouse and the old cupola of the Nachusa House can be noted in the background.

A large snowstorm was photographed from the top of the Dixon National Bank on February 10, 1944. Traffic can be seen moving slowly on South Galena Avenue. The Dixon Theatre and the Exchange Block area can be seen through the heavy snowstorm.

A clear winter's day picture taken from the roof of the Dixon National Bank shows South Galena Avenue between First and Second Streets. The photograph, taken in February, 1987, shows almost the entire block of buildings on the East side of the block.

From February 1, 1855, when the first train arrived in Dixon on the Illinois Central Railroad, until today, when an occasional freight train rumbles into town, depots have played an important part in community life. Long a center of trade and transportation, Dixon's railroad depots have served long and well. This circa 1905 view of the North Dixon Illinois Central Depot at North Brinton Avenue is a rare photograph of a building long gone from the Dixon scene. The feed mill complex across the tracks from the depot burned in 1929.

The Chicago Northwestern Railroad Depot in Dementtown was a popular arrival-departure point for over a century. This depot, razed in January, 1985, was constructed in the 1920's to replace a wooden building. A horse-driven carriage met the several passenger trains that arrived in Dixon daily for many years.

This photograph will serve to remind Dixonites of the fine passenger trains that served the city on the Chicago Northwestern Railroad for many decades. For years service to Chicago was a daily round-trip allowing passengers to leave early in the morning and return from a day's business or shopping pleasure in Chicago in the early evening. At present neither a depot nor a passenger train serves the needs of Dixonites at this location.

PETUNIA FESTIVAL

The Dixon Men's Garden Club, formed in 1950 with 26 charter members, is the organization responsible for more than 20,000 lovely petunia plants that grace the main traffic routes through the city each year from early May until late fall frost.

The Dixon Petunia Festival, a celebration of the nation's birth, is held over the July 4th weekend each year. The community event is an off-shoot of the Men's Garden Club's efforts in city beautification.

The Petunia Festival, started in 1964, annually attracts thousands of visitors to the city to enjoy the festivities as well as the beauty of the pink petunias.

Such outstanding personalities as Miss Dominion of Canada, Miss America, Miss Illinois, annual Petunia Festival Queens, an exciting Festival Parade, Sunrise Services, Drum and Bugle Corps shows, teen events, beer gardens, carnivals and other family-fun events have made the Petunia Festival very popular.

Leading political figures, local personalities, nationally known celebrities and a host of the famous and near-famous have appeared at yearly Petunia Festivals. Fireworks, ice cream socials, canoe races, talent shows — you name it, it's been seen and enjoyed at Dixon's Petunia Festival.

For 23 years, the chapters of the Beta Sigma Phi have designed and sold Dixon Petunia Festival buttons. As an integral part of the annual July 4th event, Dixon Petunia Festival buttons have become collector's items as they trace the activities of the annual Petunia Festival.

One of the highlights of the 1969 Petunia Festival was the day-long appearance of the reigning Miss America, Judi Ford of nearby Belvidere, Ill. The annual Petunia Festival Parade was more beautiful than ever that year when Miss America and 35 other beauty queens of fame and note graced the long parade route.

GALENA AVENUE FIRE

A raging fire swept through a quarter-block section of downtown Dixon along South Galena Avenue on March 1, 1962. The blaze caused more than a quarter of a million dollars in damage. Firemen fought the flames in temperatures as low as 11 degrees below zero. The United Lunch, Coppins Dixon Business College, Farmer's Mutual Fire Insurance Company of Palmyra, the offices of Attorney Morey C. Pires and the Fulmer Book Store were all considered to be almost total losses. The J.C. Penney Company store, Hank Henry's Men's Store and the Western Union office each suffered extensive damage from fire and ice.

SAUK VALLEY COLLEGE

A referendum to establish a Junior College District that would later include parts of Lee, Ogle, Whiteside, Bureau, Henry and Carroll Counties was passed on June 8, 1965. The first college board was elected in July of that year and in October approved the purchase of 163 acres of riverfront farmland midway between Dixon and Sterling on the Rock River.

In a "Name The College" contest, a 3rd grade student from St. Mary's School in Dixon named the new Junior College. The winner was Mike Flannigan and his winning entry was "Sauk Valley College."

Dr. Edward J. Sabol was named the first president of Sauk Valley College in December, 1965. A building referendum was passed to construct a 15.9 million facility. The construction of a $200,000 prefabricated building was approved and in September, 1966, Sauk Valley College opened with over 700 students.

The college continued to grow, both in programs offered and number of students served. A permanent building was constructed in 1968-70 with all programs sponsored by SVC housed in one building.

After over 20 years of service to the area, Sauk Valley College has attained a rightful place in the educational community. The college has well met its commitment "to provide a variety of educational experiences geared to meet the needs of the individual in today's complex society."

LOG CABIN

John L. Lord, president of the Lee County Old Settler's Association, first suggested the group build a permanent memorial to the early settlers of the area in the form of an old log cabin in 1894. The cabin, constructed mainly of logs taken from farms throughout the county, was located in Lloyd's Park on the grounds of the Rock River Assembly high over the Rock River in the shadow of the famed Chatauqua Park Auditorium. The log cabin was 18 by 24 feet in size with a stone fireplace and chimney. Decorated with various older mementoes of a time long past, the Old Settler's Cabin became the meeting place of annual get-togethers of the organization. Over the passing years, the cabin fell into disuse and finally, in 1968-69, efforts were made by the Lee County Historical Society to move the cabin from its 1894-1969 location to the site of the original 1832 Fort Dixon on the north side of the Rock River near the famous Lincoln-The Soldier statue. Rededication ceremonies were held August 17, 1969, for the Old Settler's Memorial Log Cabin. Each year, over the July 4th period, activities at the Log Cabin are held to remember both the Old Settlers of Lee County and the Log Cabin memorial to them.

George W. Lindquist arrived in Dixon in 1936 to begin a long career of community involvement. That career would see him serve three terms as a City Commissioner and four terms as Mayor of the City of Dixon.

The Lindquist Construction Company, founded by Andrew G. Lindquist, was hired by L.G. Rorer to build the Lee Theatre on East First Street in 1936. Lindquist's construction company was also responsible for building such Dixon structures as the Loveland Community House, additions to the KSB Hospital, Jefferson and Washington grade schools, St. Paul's Lutheran Church, Eichler's Department Store, Beier's Bakery on East River Street, F.W. Woolworth store, the remodeled Montgomery Ward store, the Dixon State School fire station, Stevenson Hospital and the Admiral Corporation building as well as many private homes and apartment structures.

George Lindquist was a supervisor at the Green River Ordinance Depot in World War II, a Director of the Illinois State Chamber of Commerce from 1952-58 and a member of the Board of Directors of the University of Dubuque for 20 years as well as acting President of the institution from December, 1969 to September, 1970. Lindquist was a founding member of the Board of Directors of the Dixon Petunia Festival in addition to being an active and ardent supporter of the annual community July 4th celebration. Active in local as well as state political affairs, George Lindquist managed several county campaigns for Senator Charles Percy. A member of the First Presbyterian Church, Lindquist served on its Session many times as well as acting as a substitute minister of the church for many years.

A devoted family man, George Lindquist and his wife, Elizabeth, have raised two daughters, Mary and Martha.

Throughout his years in Dixon, Lindquist has actively promoted industrial expansion within the community. He has served on various boards and committees charged with securing additional industry for the community and has done his share to greatly expand the industrial base of the city.

Through his long years of service to Dixon, in business, in city affairs and in the religious activities of the city, George W. Lindquist has remained an active out-going gentleman of the old school. His friendly smile and handwave as well as his greeting, "Here's my five!," along with his strong handshake are well known to Dixonites.

Dixon is far better off for having had George Lindquist in its midst.

GEORGE LINDQUIST

George and Elizabeth Lindquist were photographed standing proudly at the front door of their new home at 210 Brinton Avenue in the spring of 1940.

The first permanent office building to house the offices of District #2 of the Illinois Division of Highways was constructed at 819 Depot Avenue in 1915. Earlier offices of the District were located in the Dixon National Bank in 1917 followed by locations in the I.B. Countryman Building and the Schuler Building on West First Street. The original building contained almost 20,000 square feet of space and cost $70,000 to construct. The photograph was taken in March, 1955 when the Dementtown facility was greatly expanded.

ILLINOIS HIGHWAY BUILDING

Another building project in 1961 brought the total layout of District #2 to over three city blocks in size. This photograph, taken in 1962, shows the main entrance to the state facility that today employs over 530 people and has responsibility for twelve counties of northwest Illinois.

BEIER AND COMPANY

Beier and Company started in 1921 in Chicago under the direction of W. Earl Beier, grandson of Reinhold Beier, founder of Beier's Bakery. Beier's two sons, W.E. (Bill) Beier, Jr. and John E. Beier, took over the paper products company in 1944. In 1962, Beier and Company purchased the east end plant of the former Reynolds Wire Company then owned by the National Standard Company at 800 East River Street. The company was purchased in 1986 by Ron Bartz, who operates it today as one of Dixon's leading manufacturing concerns.

The Katherine Shaw Bethea Hospital, an 87-year-old institution in Dixon, and its newer Medical Arts Clinic companion, take excellent care of the hospital and medical needs of Dixon and the surrounding area. Grown over the years to an imposing complex of buildings and facilities, KSB Hospital continues to offer the best in health care service while acting as one of the city's largest employers.

KSB HOSPITAL

ESTHER BARTON

Born in South Dixon Township, Esther Barton lived to be over 90 years of age. Over half her life, 51 years to be exact, were spent in service to the youth of Dixon. North Dixon High School's 1912 valedictorian, she graduated from Northern Illinois College, DeKalb in 1916. Esther Barton began her teaching career as a teacher at the E.C. Smith School in 1916. She later became principal of that school, principal of the Woodworth School from 1936 to 1938 and principal at the newly constructed Lincoln School from the day it opened until 1967. Esther Barton was a 25-year member of the Dixon Park Board and received the Freedom Foundation's Educator's Award medal in 1960. Barton was widely traveled and donated many of the artifacts she gathered from around the world to the Loveland Community House Museum. The Dixon educator attended classes at 15 different colleges and universities over the years, was an active member of several local and national clubs, organizations and societies and held the honor of being Dixon's first fully licensed aviatrix. Esther Barton died June 9, 1986, leaving behind a life-long legend of accomplishment not soon to be repeated.

WINSTON MCREYNOLDS

Winston McReynolds was born in Henderson, Tennessee, where he lived until the age of 10. At this time, his father moved his family north to Dixon where "Wink" attended public schools and graduated from North Dixon High School. An outstanding student and athlete, McReynolds later graduated from Lane College, Jackson, Tennessee. He became a teacher in Paris, Tennessee but grew disillusioned with racial practices in the south. Wink returned to Dixon where he was employed by Commonwealth Edison for 31 years. He served on the Dixon Park Board and had charge of Reynolds' Field where he was instrumental in securing lights for night baseball at that location. Wink McReynolds was active in community affairs, became an assistant township supervisor and was the first black to be elected to the Lee County Board. Appointed to the Lee County Housing Authority, he became its chairman and carried out expansion plans for scattered site housing in Dixon. A member of the NAACP as well as the Second Baptist Church, Winston McReynolds was active in securing a high rise facility for senior citizens; a facility named in his honor in 1975.

DIXON NATIONAL BANK CENTENNIAL

Celebrating "A Century of Service", the Dixon National Bank in September, 1971, invited the greater Dixon area community to a week-long birthday celebration. Events included two nights of old time movies at the Dixon Theatre, colorful decorations and displays, costumes of the era, a Sunday Open House that attracted a crowd estimated to be in the thousands and the release of a special limited edition historical publication. The first century of service to the Dixon area was well celebrated by the Dixon National Bank; a fact that will be attested to by those who took part in the gala affair.

Dixon National Bank officers, dressed in the attire of a century ago, posed for this picture during the 1971 Centennial celebration. From left to right they are: H.O. Lovett, John W. Kuster, Donald R. Lovett, James P. Green, Robert W. Castle, William E. Reigle, Eileen Law and Leo B. Miller.

RONALD REAGAN

The motion picture career of Dixon's Ronald "Dutch" Reagan was followed closely by Dixonites. As each of his movies were shown at either the Dixon or Lee Theatres, Reagan's local fans turned out to applaud their hero.

Ronald Reagan's return visits to his hometown were varied and many. He addressed the Dixon High School honors banquet in April, 1963, and made political campaign visits to Dixon in 1976 and 1980. In August, 1978, Ronald Reagan attended the 50th Reunion of his 1928 high school graduating class from North Dixon High School.

Reagan's political star rose with his election as Governor of California for two terms and his national quest for the office of President of the United States in 1976 and 1980. As "Dutch" Reagan gained in national prominence, all residents of Dixon had reason for deep satisfaction and community pride.

His election as President of the United States on November 4, 1980 gave Dixonites reason to hold one of the largest celebrations ever staged in the community. When the 1980 election results were in, "Dutch" Reagan received an overwhelming 5,755 votes from Dixon's 20 precincts.

To honor President Reagan on his 73rd birthday in Dixon, a

In 1976, Ronald Reagan unsuccessfully sought the nomination of the Republican Party for the office of President of the United States. His gallant struggle and gentleman-like acceptance of his loss made him a force to be reckoned with four years later.

The boyhood home of Ronald "Dutch" Reagan at 816 S. Hennepin Avenue was built in 1891. It was the Reagan family home from 1920 to 1924. The home is under the watchful eye of the local Ronald Reagan Home Restoration Preservation Association and has been restored to its appearance inside and out as the early 20's home of the Reagan family.

full program of activities was scheduled including the dedication of his 816 S. Hennepin Avenue boyhood home. Highlighting the affair was the presence of President and Mrs. Reagan, his brother Neil and a host of other dignitaries.

President Reagan's election to a second term in November, 1984, once again signaled the start of an evening celebration all citizens of Dixon will long remember.

The people of Dixon and the greater Dixon vicinity haven't lost their idealistic conception of their favorite son. To most of them, the President of the United States, Ronald Wilson Reagan, will always be remembered as "Dutch" Reagan, the likeable small town boy who made good.

Upon his election in 1980 as President of the United States, many Dixonites received copies of this official White House photograph taken by Jack Knightlinger.

Hundreds of Dixonites gathered on Galena Avenue to wish their President a speedy recovery from gunshot wounds suffered at the hands of a would-be assassin.

South Galena Avenue, looking north over the Rock River, has been Dixon's main north/south thoroughfare down through the years. This photograph, taken from East Second Street in the early 1960's, shows a busy avenue lined with automobiles and retail stores.

First Street, in this 1960's era photograph taken from Peoria Avenue looking East, was a busy downtown center of retail shopping. Through the passing years, First Street has been the hub of Dixon's thriving retail and professional activities.

PETUNIA FESTIVAL PARADE

The 1987 Dixon Petunia Festival Parade was led by the Dixon Police Department Honor Guard. Seen crossing the Ronald Reagan Bridge on Peoria Avenue, the Honor Guard led a 130 unit parade that highlighted the annual community Petunia Festival.

LEE COUNTY COURTS BUILDING

Constructed in 1985, the Lee County Courts Building holds the district court facilities and is located directly across South Galena Avenue from the Lee County Courthouse.

LEE COUNTY LAW ENFORCEMENT BUILDING

The Lee County Law Enforcement Building, constructed in 1970-71, was the first shared-use building of its kind in the State of Illinois. Built on the site of the old Lee County Jail that had served since 1872, the building houses the administrative function of the county's sheriff's department serves as the headquarters of the Dixon Police Department and contains the complete correctional and detention facilities for Lee County.

DIXON FAMILY YMCA

In the early 1960's, the Dixon YMCA was reactivated under the guidance and direction of Henry M. Hey, Edward A. Lawton, Jr. and other interested community leaders. In 1965, a major fund drive was successfully undertaken to raise the money necessary to later construct a full service building facility. Ronald "Dutch" Reagan, a member of the Dixon YMCA in the 1920's, was one of the first contributors to the new YMCA Building Fund. The Dixon Family YMCA, located on North Galena Avenue between the Rock River and East Boyd Street, has now gained a firm and rightful place in the life of the Dixon area community.

CITY BANK

The City Bank, located on South Galena Avenue, underwent extensive remodeling and enlargement during 1986-87. The addition of drive-through facilities off Galena Avenue through a park-like area is just one of the many new features of the banking facility.

FIRST FEDERAL SAVINGS AND LOAN

The First Federal Savings and Loan Association, begun in Dixon in 1960, has grown with the community. Alden F. Hunter, first president of the organization together with Dorothy Butler, longtime secretary-manager of the business, had their first business address in Dixon at 119 South Galena Avenue. A few years later First Federal moved to offices on West First Street and in the 1970's established themselves in a new and modern facility at the corner of North Galena Avenue and West Chamberlin Street.

POST SCRIPT

One clear and understandable thread is interwoven throughout the fabric of Dixon's long and interesting history. This filament, which has remained steadfast and true for 157 years, concerns the role of community leadership.

The reader has but to scan the pages of Dixon's history to see that beginning with "Father" Dixon in 1830, community leaders have surfaced to become dominant in the growth and progress of the community. Often the heavy reigns of leadership have been held by one pair of hands but more often the weight has been shared by several strong hands.

These leaders of the community have come from the ranks of business and industry, from the halls of education or from the quiet solitude of religious endeavor. Some have been entrepreneurs, some have been motivated by politics, while others have led the community from the fields of medicine, finance or civic involvement.

Dixon National Bank - North. Located on North Galena Avenue, the banking facility is the epitome of modern financial service.

The Howell Park bench overlooking the Rock River is a popular resting place for young and old alike. It honors Edward Nelson Howell, President of the Dixon Park Board from 1903 to 1929.

The Goodyear Blimp "America" landed at the Dixon Municipal Airport on August 26, 1986 and departed the next day, after being viewed by thousands of interested local citizens.

Each generation of Dixonites has contributed its share of leaders. Some were native born while others were residents of Dixon by choice.

But no matter how these leaders led, no matter how they choose to serve, lead and serve each one did and to the very best of their individual ability.

Whenever Dixon needed leadership, that leadership surfaced and manifested itself in a firm and positive manner. When the community tended to become complacent, leadership was present to make sure that complacency didn't become firmly entrenched. When industrial, commercial or educational endeavors lagged, community leadership was present to recharge the spirit of Dixon.

Strong, positive, effective community leaders are a tangible trademark of Dixon. All through its history the city has been guided by those whose interest in the betterment of the community has made it what it is today — a fine place to live, a good place to work, and a place we are proud to call home.

Lisa Lovett and her dog, Crockett, are to be seen in front of the Tri County Animal Shelter on North Galena Avenue in the summer of 1987.

Ray Neisewander, President of Raynor Manufacturing Company, Dixon, is shown here with Raynor Motorsports racing car and its driver. The Raynor Garage Door vehicle was entered in the prestigious Indianapolis Memorial Day 500 in 1987.

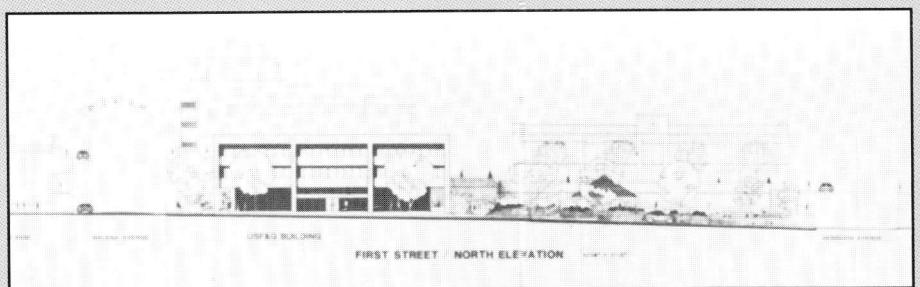

The proposed United States Fidelity and Guaranty Company office-parking-retail complex shows great promise of being a giant step forward for the downtown Dixon area. This architect's conception of the USF&G project displays the beautiful building's location on S. Galena Avenue and W. First Street.

ACKNOWLEDGEMENTS

In the Preface to *Historical Reminiscenses,* the following quotation from another author was noted:

> "In its preparation, sources of information have been sought and appropriations freely made from presumably authentic data. No claim is made to originality and numerous mistakes will doubtless be discovered, especially by those disposed to be hypercritical."

I could not begin to express in better words than these the thoughts that I have had in writing this book. I would hope those who have helped me will know how very much I appreciate their every assistance.

To William E. Shaw, publisher of the *Dixon Telegraph,* the entire staff of the Dixon Public Library (and especially to Janet Sanders for her love of Dixon history), the kind people connected with the Loveland Community House Museum and the Lee County Historical Society and those who shared their personal photographs for our viewing, I am very much in debt.

Robert E. Nellis, former Editor of the *Dixon Evening Telegraph,* in the late 1960's encouraged me to record local history on the pages of the newspaper for which he was then responsible. Without the constant encouragement of Bob Nellis those many years ago, this current effort would not have been possible.

A large dose of special thanks is extended to Donald R. Lovett, John Kuster, Bud and Mary Ellen Wilson and Stella Grobe for their outstanding dedication to the success of the book. Jeffrey A. Lovett's photographic expertise combined with his deep and abiding devotion to local history is especially appreciated, respected and admired.

And, last but certainly not least, a very big thank you to my wife, Marilyn, for her constant encouragement, devotion and love.

ADVISORY COMMITTEE

George Lamb, Author   John W. Kuster   C. "Bud" Wilson

Stella Grobe   Jeffrey A. Lovett   Mary Ellen Wilson

BIBLIOGRAPHY

A Century of Service, Dixon National Bank, 1971.

Barge, William D., *Early Lee County*, 1918.

Brown, S.M., *Memories of the Northern Illinois Normal School And Dixon Business College*, 1938-1939.

Dixon Sun, numerous issues, 1872 to end of publication.

Dixon Pilot Association Aviation Annual, 1973

Dixon Telegraph: Half Century Edition, 1901. Centennial Edition, 1951. Dynamic Decade Edition, 1970. Heritage Edition, 1976. Numerous other issues, 1851-1987.

Historical Encyclopedia of Illinois, Bateman & Selby.

"Historical Reminiscences," George Lamb. *Dixon Evening Telegraph*, March 1968 - December 1968.

History of Dixon And Palmyra. Dixon Evening Telegraph Print, 1880.

History of Lee County. H.H. Hill & Company, 1881.

Johnson, Dana C. *A Souvenir of Dixon - The New England City*, 1896.

Johnson, Stanley N. *Dixon Post Office - A Brief History*, 1984.

Keister, Phillip L. *The Sterling, Dixon and Eastern Electric Railway*, 1963.

Lamb, George. *Historical Reminiscences*, 1970.

Lamb, George. *Historical Yearbook*, 1972, 1973, 1974.

"Looking Back." George Lamb. *Dixon Evening Telegraph*, 1987.

Recollections of the Pioneers of Lee County. Lee County Columbian Club, 1893.

Souvenir of the Association of the Illinois National Guard And Naval Reserve - Dixon, Illinois, 1909.

Stevens, Frank E. *The Black Hawk War*.

"We Remember When." George Lamb. *Dixon Evening Telegraph*, June 1981 - December 1982.

"Yesteryear." George Lamb. *Dixon Evening Telegraph*, February 1971 - March 1972.

Zinnen, Tom. *Institutions of Higher Learning in Lee County*, 1977.

Zinnen, Tom. *The Shoe Industry in Dixon*, 1975.

PHOTOGRAPH CREDITS

Deep appreciation is extended to those who contributed photographs and materials for inclusion in DIXON: A PICTORIAL HISTORY. Without their deep interest in the success of this project, it would not have been possible to publish such an extensive collection of Dixon's colorful history. Contributors were:

Dorothy Allen
Winona Angier
Betty Beanblossom
Ed Blackburn
Peter L. Blackburn
Ida Borell
Dorothy Butler
Gertrude Carpenter
Robert W. Castle
Henry Chamness
Terry Coffey
Harold "Barney" Coss
Florence Daehler
Mr. & Mrs. James Dishman
Dixon Camera Center
Dixon Chamber of Commerce
Dixon Fire Department
Helen M. Dixon
Dixon High School
Mr. & Mrs. James Dixon
Dixon National Bank
Alvah Drew
Verda Feldkirchner
Delores Ferger

Marian Floto
Dorothy Fraza
Robert Gehant
Mr. & Mrs. Edward Gerdes
Forrest L. Grobe
Mr. & Mrs. Kenneth Grobe
Frances Hemminger
Francis Hepfer
Hey Brothers, Inc.
Pat Higgs
Hope Hinds
Robert Hintz
Illinois Department of Transportation
Marilyn Kitzmiller
Mr. & Mrs. Everett Kraft
Milton Kosuma
John W. Kuster
Patrick S. Lamb
Nancy Lillyman
Diane Markel
Jane Marshall
John McLane
Millie McNinch
Mary Mobarek

Nancy Morrissey
Delores Owen
Katherine Pettenger
Dr. Harry Quick
Raynor Manufacturing, Inc.
Elwood C. Rickard
Robert V. Reed
Frances Reeverts
Mr. & Mrs. Charles Roundy
Stephen B. Saathoff
Louis F. Salzman
Gilbert Scheffler
Joyce Scheffler
Mr. & Mrs. Thomas Schmidt
Mrs. Lawrence Schott
Dr. and Mrs. Greg Selgestad
Dan Shiaras
Lawrence Slick
Mrs. Edward Sorbe
John St. Clair
Mrs. William Steder
Evelyn Street
Debra S. Sutton
Herman Thompson
Jerry Trotter

Norris Tucker
Thomas Van Matre
Louis Venier
Mr. & Mrs. Robert Vest
Ted Wallin
Walter C. Knack Co.
Lucille Watson
Robert Warner
Mr. & Mrs. Dale Weidman
John R. Wernick
Orville Westgor
Estate of Esther Whitcombe
Paul Whitcombe
Mr. & Mrs. C. "Bud" Wilson
Harold Witzleb
Wilson Woodrow
Edward Worley
Dixon Evening Telegraph Collection
Dixon Public Library Collection
Loveland Community Museum Collection
Jeffrey A. Lovett Collection

INDEX

Abbott, John P., 161
Abbott, Charles, 30
Ackerman, Wayne, 164
Alexander, Philip M., 38, 39, 66
Ames, W. David, 34
Anders, Ronald, 160
Andrus, Leonard, 24, 57, 60
Appleford, J.D., 71
Arthus, Edwin, 148
Atherton, I.W., 15
Atkins, Louis B., 28
Atkinson, Henry, 12
Auman, Earl, 150
Ayers, Jason C., 28, 51, 114

—B—
Balen, Bill, 124
Bales, John, 75
Barr, James B., 10
Bailey, Harry, 114
Barge, William, 91
Bardwell, A.C., 17, 86, 97
Barlow, Abner, 138
Barton, Esther, 135, 153, 167, 186
Baum, W.D., 156
Baux, Dwain, 161
Beanblossom, Willard, 134, 143
Becker, Henry, 52, 55, 66
Beggs, John J., 102
Beier Family, 50, 69, 108, 109, 126, 172, 183, 185
Benjamin, Andrew, 66
Bennett, Edward, 142
Bethea, Solomon H., 68, 80
Bevilacqua, Tony, 169
Bevis, Philip, 28
Bishop, Myrtle, 148
Blackburn, Ed, 100
Black Hawk, 8, 10, 11, 12
Blades, Carl, 164
Boardman, Thaddeus, 19, 52, 66
Bogardus, John L., 10
Bovey, Elias, 50
Bovey, J and Son, 55
Bovey, Robert, 142
Bowman and Boardman, 40
Bowman Brothers, 134
Bowman, Samuel M., 16, 21
Boyton and Richards, 133
Brewster, E.H., 84
Brinton, William B., 69, 99, 112
Brooks and Daily, 24
Brooks, J.B., 18, 38, 52
Brooks, Noah, 12, 16
Brush, C.E., 97
Buchanan, Mary, 167
Buckaloo, Al, 142
Buckaloo, Elizabeth, 129
Bull, M.P., 17
Burdick, Henry, 138
Burket, John N., 41
Burkitt, Cleve, 171
Butler, C.G., 21

—C—
Cahill, Helen M., 166
Cahill, M., 75
Cahill, William, 72

Campbell, Edward, 124
Campbell, Thomas, 21
Camp, Elizabeth, 91
Camp, James I., 66
Carner, Ruth, 135
Castle, Robert W., 186
Chammess, Henry, 109
Chandler, Leo, 164
Chapman, Frank, 177
Charters Family, 15, 18, 28, 58
Cheverton, Harry, 46
Christ, Steve, 160
Clears, James D., 62
Coffey, Agnes A., 129
Coffey, Thomas, 94, 95
Coleman, John, 44
Cook, Eva M., 129
Cooley, O.W., 35
Coss Family, 69, 150
Countryman Family, 44, 70, 74, 184
Cowles, Perry, 72
Crabtree, Judge, 76
Crabtree, J.D., 59
Crawford, Joseph, 15, 44, 51
Crunelle, Leonard, 135
Cropsey, John H., 27
Cumins, Theron, 27, 57, 60, 68, 91, 104
Curtis, Charles W., 24
Curtis, E.R., 30
Curtis, W.W., 30

—D—
Davies, T.G., 92
Davis, Ross M., 99
Dayton, E.E., 69
Deere, John, 24, 27, 60
Dement, Henry D., 24, 57
Dement, John, 11, 14, 19, 24, 28, 52, 57, 63, 102
DePuy, James, 18, 41
Devine, Leander A., 66
Devine, W.P., 28
Dey, Henry S., 28
Dille, J.B., 37
Dixon, Elizabeth A., 65
Dixon, F.F., 73
Dixon, George C., 133, 135
Dixon, Henry S., 97
Dixon, James P., 10, 19
Dixon, "Father" John, 10, 11, 12, 13, 16, 18, 21, 22, 26, 32, 38, 82, 97, 135, 166, 194
Dixon, John W., 50, 65
Dixon, Rebecca, 8, 19, 65
Dixon, Sherwood, 44, 166
Dodd, LeRoy, 164
Dodge, Orris B., 60, 68, 91, 140
Donaldson, H.E., 78, 79
Downing, George J., 69
Draper, Kay, 172
Drew, W.D., 103
Duffy, John W., 69, 117
Duffy, Molly, 167
Durkes, Warren C., 44

—E—
Edelmann, E.E., 172
Edsall, James K., 16
Edwards, I. Frank, 37, 86, 97
Edwards, Lew E., 30
Eells, Samuel C., 44, 57
Eichler Family, 68, 75, 134, 183
Eller and Willey, 134
Ely, Quartus, 28, 66
Emerson, C.F., 68
Emmerson, Louis, 135
Espy, Robert H., 144
Eustace, John V., 15, 17, 28, 30, 58
Everett, Oliver, 10, 15, 26, 87
Evett, Edward D., 105

—F—
Fargo, C.H., 42, 68, 126
Fazzi, E.L. "Babe", 134
Ferguson, Albert, 27
Ferguson, E.J., 122
Finch, Ferris, 21, 26, 30, 66
Fisher, H.V., 92
Fisk, Charles R., 11, 17
Fitzgerald, James, 41
Fitzsimmons, Royal, 142
Flannigan, Mike, 181
Flint, John C., 37
Floto, Clifford, 148
Ford, John E., 117
Fordyce, Albert, 160
Frazer, B.J., 153
Frerichs, Albert, 113
Frye, R.R., 105
Fulfs, Harry and Walter, 69

—G—
Gardner, Frank, 149
Garland, Joseph A., 161
Garrison, W.S., 30
Gearhart, O.I., 69
Giesenheimer, Anna, 44
Gilbraith, Smith, 10, 38
Glasgow, C.J., 172
Glessner, Elwin, 134
Godfrey, Charles, 11, 27, 52
Godfrey, William H., 18
Goeke, O.F., 69
Goral, Matt and Chet, 134
Gorgas, A.B., 27
Green, E.M. "Cotton", 172
Green, James P., 186
Greig and Baum, 97
Groehling, Alex, 148
Grove, Lawrence, 149

—H—
Haistenberg, Ab, 164
Halstead, Ethel, 129
Hamilton, Jude W., 10
Hank Henry, 172, 181
Hansen, F.W., 161
Harney, William S., 12
Harrison, B.W., 134
Harsha, W.W., 8, 35, 40
Harshbarger, Clarence, 164

Hart, Leon, 110
Havens, Sarah, 61
Hawkins, Rev. and Mrs., 125
Haynes, Francis, 111
Henderson, C.M., 42, 68, 72, 126
Hey Family, 69, 155, 170
Hey, Henry, W., 150
Higgins, Henry C., 102
Higgins, W.B., 37
Hine, E.W., 10
Hintz, Harry, 103, 148
Hoban, Thomas, 28
Hoefer, Mrs. I.B., 161
Hollbrook, Eugene, 160
Hollenbeck, Jerome, 44
Hoon, John, 148
Hooper, O.F., 17
Hopkins, Mason, 150
Horner, Flora, 148
Horton, Claude, 103
Horton, D.S., 99
Howell, Edward N., 38, 86, 194
Howell, George L., 38
Howell and Sullivan, 31
Hoyle, Dorothy, 135
Huffman Family, 134
Hughes, Charles H., 84, 85, 86, 105
Hunter, Alden F., 44

—I—
Ives, Clinton "Pete", 148
Ives, George, 153

—J—
Jarvis, James, 148
Jenks, H.B., 28
Jerome and Downing, 27, 63
Johnson, Dava C., 105
Johnson, Oscar, 103, 134
Johnson, Samuel L., 10
Johnson, Verne, 150
Johnson, W.N., 28, 87
Jones, Royal, 68
Jones, William "Billy", 63
Julian, John, 75
Jurgens, Clara, 90

—K—
Kaye, Mabel, 129
Keeley, W.R., 161
Kelchner, Earl, 161
Kerz Family, 134, 160
Ketchin, Ken, 148
Kirk, David, 149
Klavohn, Jack K., 160
Klingman, Olive, 168
Kling, Olive, 168
Kling, E.L., 30, 70
Knack, Walter C., 69, 149
Kock, Charles, 149
Kriem, Frank, 69
Kump, Ruth, 155
Kuster, John, 187

—L—
LaFever, Ronnie, 164
Laing Family, 25, 134, 143
Lancaster, A.H., 134

198

Lane, Charles, 16
LaPorte, Pierre, 10
LaSallier, 10
Law, Eileen, 187
Lawton Brothers, 134, 150, 151
LeBlanc, Robert, 171
Lennon, J. Barry, 133
Leydig, Eurith, 170
Lincoln, Abraham, 12, 13, 18, 26, 32, 58, 134, 135
Lindquist Family, 121, 134, 154, 183
Little and Brooks, 14
Little, Joseph T., 14, 27, 38
Little, Thomas, 27
Logan, Max, 150
Lord, John L., 182
Loveland Family, 38, 68, 154, 167
Lovett Family, 44, 187, 195
Lowell Family, 69, 58, 86
Lucas, H.S., 28
Luckey, Zachariah, 21, 47

—M—
Madden, N.H., 155
Mall, Ken, 142
Malloy, Edward, 75
Manifici, Emil, 148
Manning, E.T., 40
Marshall, C., 134
Massey, Vernon and Gladys, 38
Mattox, John, 27
McAlpine, William J., 97, 120, 140
McClanahan, Frank, 138
McKenney Family, 10, 11, 14, 22, 92, 129
McIntyre, Frank, 169
McReynolds, Winston, 186
Mead, J.C., 28
Mead, Leona, 27
Mercer, Don, 164
Mercer, Mike, 170
Meyers, Clarence, 149
Miller, Charles, 133
Miller, J.E., 103
Miller, Leo B., 187
Miller, T.J., 55
Moeller, Theodore, 28
Moore, J.H., 27
Morrison, Almond E., 170
Morrison, Herbert, 28
Morse and Benjamin, 27
Moyer, John, 141
Murphy, Edward S., 18
Murphy, Mrs. David, 18
Murphy, Melvin, 134
Mullery, Greg, 171

—N—
Nash, J.B., 44
Nattress, Edna, 134
Neisewander, Ray, 195
Nelson, Irene, 107
Nettz, George, 110, 111
Newberry, J.J., 172
Newcomer, F.X., 68
Nichols, H.H., 21
Noble, Charles, R., 60

Noble and Hollenbeck, 44
Noble, Silas, 44
Noble, Henry T., 27, 37, 44, 57, 60

—O—
Ogee Family, 10, 12
O'Malley, George, 142
O'Malley, Pete, 161
Ortt, E.K., 69
Orvis Family, 24, 57
Oswalt, George and Gary, 171
Owen, Andy, 135

—P—
Paine, Henry E., 75
Page, George H., 68, 100, 150
Pankhurst, Besse C., 129
Parsons, C.D., 83
Parsons, E.C., 87
Parsons, Louella, 162
Patrick, S.G., 15
Peterson, Carl and Betty, 134
Phelps, John, 21
Pitts, Alexander, 54
Pierce, Edmund, 172
Pitcher, L.D., 70, 133
Pires, Morey C., 181
Platt and Son, 27
Plein, Nicholas, 62
Plotkin, Jack, 160
Porter, Jerome, 11
Potts, Paul, 169
Pratt, Frank M., 107
Pratt, Henry, 134
Pratt, J.H., 27
Pratt and Reed, 106, 107
Prince, Earl, 150, 151

—R—
Randall, Frank, 134
Read and Burright, 93, 155
Reagan Family, 69, 123, 130, 134, 159, 162, 163, 172, 188
Reed, Kirby J., 106, 107
Reed and Son, 68
Reigle, William E., 187
Reynolds Family, 68, 83, 84, 85, 105, 126, 134, 140, 172, 185, 186
Rex, Charles, 93
Rice, Curtis, 148
Rickard, E.H., 115, 120
Rickert, Clark, 142
Roberts, Hal, 134
Robinson, John, 11, 12, 33
Robinson, R.P., 27
Robertson and Eastman, 44
Roberts and McKay, 27
Roe, Benny, 164
Rogers and Owen, 172
Rorer, L.G., 120, 121, 134, 183
Rosbrook and Wasley, 92
Ross, C.W., 69
Routh, Carlton, 155
Royster, Barry, 172
Ruffin, Thomas, 171
Ruthruff, John M., 90
Ryan, Courtney, 134
Ryan, E.J., 73

—S—
Sabol, Edward J., 172, 181
Salsbury, D.G., 21
Salzman, John, 77, 104
Salzman, Ralph, 134
Samuelson, Sam, 148
Schertner, James, 160
Scholl, Edith, 167
Schorr, George, 62
Schnell, Reinhardt, 139
Schuler Family, 44, 50, 68, 69, 70, 113, 138, 184
Schumard, Aggie, 142
Scott, Winfield, 13
Scudder, C.O., 27
Senneff and Drew, 150
Shaw, Alonzo, 17
Shaw Family, 11, 17, 42, 50, 66, 71, 80, 91, 141, 165
Shaw, G.H.T., 105
Sinow and Wieman, 134
Skellenger, George, 12
Slothower, William V., 160
Smith, Charles, G., 86
Smith, Eli C., 27, 35, 37
Smith, E.W., 104
Smith, Scott, 171
Snyder, Ben, 155
Sorge, Mrs. Edward, 119
Spencer, Harold, 148
Spencer, Lester, 164
Squires, George, 68
Stanfield, Sam, 134
Steinman, C.A., 36
Stephans, Harry, 172
Stephens, Dr., 77
Stephens, H., 142
Sterling, Robert, 30
Stevens, H.J., 59
Stevens, H.U., 99
Stevens, W.D., 59
Stevenson, J.E., 12
Stiles and Eddy, 11
Stiles, Elias B., 15, 16, 28, 30, 44, 54
Stoddard, A.H., 36
Street, Lester C., 129
Stripe, Norman, 160
Strohm, Mae, 129
Surman, H.F., 69
Sugg, L.A., 40

—T—
Tennant, Vernon, 106
Thomann, C.H., 62
Thomas, A.U., 71
Thomas, Clara, 123
Thomas, John V., 105
Thomas, Wayne, 160
Thompson, Conrad, 62
Thompson, H., 11, 22
Tillison, Alanzo, 105
Timmons, Larry, 75
Todd, W.M., 24, 57
Toor, H.O., 172
Trautwein, Forrest J., 105
Trevane, Henry, 75
Trein, Will, 55, 68
Trippeer, Mrs. J.O., 143
Truesdell, L.E., 47

Trumbull, Lyman, 21
Truman, Frederick A., 27, 59
Turner, Alex, 47

—U—
Underwood, Nathan Jr., 28, 52
Utley, Joseph, 44, 57

—V—
Vann and Means, 28
Van Bibber, John D., 90
Van Epps Family, 76
Van Epps, W.E., 30
Vaile, Edward, 86, 142
Vaile, Morrison, 89

—W—
Wadsworth, Douglas, 164
Wadsworth, E.S., 161
Wakely, Tom, 171
Walgreen Family, 68, 69, 99, 138, 139, 153, 172
Ware, William H. "Billy", 68
Watson, Frank, 42, 126
Watts, James E., 37
Webb, H., 28
Webb, Rogers and Woodruff, 14
Weber Family, 150
Webster, Charles, 171
Walty, David, 66
Wendel, George O., 28, 55
Westgor, Orville, 148
Wheeler, H.O., 73
Wheeler, Ozias, 66
Whitcombe, Esther J., 113
Wilson, Hannah, 84
Wilson, John, 10, 21
Williams, C.P., 152
Williams, George, 114
Williams, Martin H., 66
Willett, Charles K., 134, 172
Wingert, Edward E., 37
Wood, Alonzo, 30
Wood, Lorenso, 61
Woolworth, F.W., 69, 134, 172, 183
Wynn, May, 91
Wynn, W.W., 56, 75

—Y—
Yarney and Gilman, 30
Yeast, Carroll, 149
Youngren, Mark, 171

—Z—
Zeien, Herbert, 134

199

Quotation from *Where's The Rest Of Me,* Ronald Reagan, 1965.

"All of us have a place to go back to; Dixon is that place for me."

RONALD WILSON REAGAN

40TH PRESIDENT OF THE UNITED STATES OF AMERICA